The Palm

THE PALM

A GUIDE TO YOUR HIDDEN POTENTIAL

Rita Robinson

NEWCASTLE PUBLISHING CO., INC.
North Hollywood, California
1988

Copyright © 1988 by Rita Robinson
All rights reserved.
ISBN 0-87877-133-6

Illustrated by Nell Blackwell
Edited by Janrae Frank and Douglas Menville
Cover/Book Design by Riley K. Smith
Back cover photo by Haila Hardage

FIRST EDITION
A NEWCASTLE BOOK
First printing, April 1988
10 9 8 7 6 5 4 3 2
Printed in the United States of America

Acknowledgments

MY APPRECIATION TO Nell Blackwell for bringing this book together with her artistic talents, and to Janrae Frank and Doug Menville for their copious hours of editing, which greatly improved the book's final outcome. Special thanks to Wrightwood, California artist Haila Hardage for the photo of me appearing on the back cover.

To RUTH DEVER

for her loving and ceaseless encouragement,

and to my children
Dawson, Julie and Jenny,
who add sparkle to my life.

Contents

Foreword

I HAVE ATTEMPTED TO LEARN palm reading from books several times in the past, but always met with frustration because my own palm is seemingly filled with every possible line and its variation. My hands are a mass of details such as forks, stars, islands, grilles, and crosses—with nothing definite to make sense of.

Now Rita Robinson has presented the palm in such a way that I am finally able to build my impressions, first from an overall view—such as you might ascertain at a glance upon meeting someone, or by observing their hands in a good photograph—down to the minute particulars that are important in order to refine the overall impression. By seeing the whole first, then slowly integrating the details, and with the aid of her specific illustrations and numerous examples, my palm makes sense to me at long last.

Rita has provided us with an exceptionally clear, commonsense explanation of not only the hand, but also why we would want to understand what it means. As a guide or roadmap of our potential, we can gain a clearer sense of our personal destinations and the varieties of ways we can get there. As she points out, roadblocks and barriers become interesting detours that allow us to develop our less-used abilities and even create alternate possibilities, causing lines to actually change as we change. Thus, at least to some extent, we re-draw the map as we live life, and meet the challenges.

To Rita all hands have their value. No single characteristic is bad, only more or less extreme, and while she explains the excesses and problems, she focuses on the potentials and affirms the qualities that can be accessed. Demonstrated by descriptions from six countries of the "ideal" feminine hand, she shows that beauty in hands is a cultural preference. She prefers the "useful, purposeful hand," filled with character and will, but adds that "beautiful hands needn't be a drawback."

In basing her information not only on the traditions and practice of palmistry but also on thorough examination of contemporary research by psychologists and health professionals, Rita Robinson offers a sensible and practical guide to understanding your no-longer-hidden potential. And just as integrating the factors in the hand is the key to interpretation, so too, integrating this interpretation with the will to actualize your potential is the key to making the most of your life.

MARY K. GREER
San Francisco
January, 1988

Introduction

THE PALM IS a personal guide to human potential. The unique shape, texture and movement of the hands, plus the many lines that cover the palm like the map to a hidden treasure, reveal the past, present and future of an individual's journey through life. Some of these discoveries may cause uneasiness. Other characteristics, perhaps long buried in the trauma of growing up and trying to fit into society, may be uncovered and shed glorious light into a person's life.

By understanding the significance of the hand's markings, we can become aware of our mental and physical strengths and weaknesses, likes and dislikes, capabilities and faults and inborn temperaments. We can then use this knowledge to our advantage.

This outline, or guide, as shown in the hands, is neither infallible nor unchanging because, like a road map, it shows many ways to proceed toward our destinations. During this journey of life, we may, in fact, decide to change or alter our course, and new lines may appear. But regardless of these changes, the guide is with us to use to our journey's end.

If we treat the map as a friend, we can use the talents and capabilities it shows to their fullest, because when we come to a roadblock, we can plainly see the other routes available to us.

The obstacles we encounter may come in the guise of interfering friends, lovers or relatives; problems with work, success, careers; barriers that make us change direction; health problems; or our own real or imagined fears.

But the hand also shows us our strengths. As Walt Whitman, 19th-century American poet, wrote:

> I am larger, better than I thought.
> I did not know I held so much goodness.

For this reason, I usually look for individual qualities such as vitality and energy in a person's hand before I search further for inherent talent.

People tend to forget that talent only accounts for five percent of what they can achieve; ninety-five percent is the result of hard work and drive.

I once interviewed a thirty-eight-year-old woman who was head of her class in law school. She had always wanted to be an attorney, but her high school had said her IQ wasn't high enough.

"They didn't take into consideration the drive I have," she said. "Well, I have it, and I'm going to be an attorney—even if I did have to wait a few years."

Unlike the attorney, few of us are really acquainted with ourselves. We have no direction in life, aren't aware of our deeply ingrained likes and dislikes. We rush into the first job that offers a decent amount of money, or into a marriage brought about by the heat of the moment.

We're trying to be round pegs in square holes.

A friend of mine, a Los Angeles therapist named Paul Hilsdale, has a picture of a tree in his office. The portion of the tree above ground is a beautiful growing thing, but the roots of the tree are also shown beneath the ground. We should be aware that the roots are there, but not allow them to surface and destroy the beauty of the tree. Nonetheless, we need to nourish the entire tree so that it blooms magnificently.

Palmistry is like that tree, in that we can use the information it imparts to nourish our souls as we grow, always being mindful of our roots.

We are more than we think we are, and the palm gives us clues to hidden talent, desires, strengths and capabilities.

While reading the hands of a twenty-six-year-old woman who had four children from a marriage that began at the age of fifteen, I heard her lament that her hand had no Line of Fate—a sign of people who just sort of drift through life and live at the caprice of others. But other markings pointed out strong characteristics.

Her hand also indicated a second marriage and a happier time of it after age forty. What didn't show was that her first husband would commit suicide, which he did, forcing her out into the working world, where she would find the strong and sturdy stuff of which she was made.

Years later, when I attended her second wedding, we noted that a Line of Fate had formed—not in the more common place, but in the middle of her palm, indicating that she had developed the capacity to take control in the second half of her life.*

In this sense, palmistry is a form of divination, but in itself, can only go so far. Palmistry cannot tell you the exact job you will accept at a certain point in your life, the precise location of where you will live or specifically who you will marry.

It can, however, tell you such things as the type of work you're best suited for, when you will make career changes, when you will move (if the trip changes your style of life) and the type of person you're likely to marry (based on your own characteristics).

There are exceptions, however. A friend of mine was once told by a palmist that he would move to California and go to work for the movie studios on a specific date. Sometime later, this happened, exactly as predicted!

When palmists are able to give specific dates, places and names, they are combining palmistry with clairvoyance. There is nothing wrong with this. They are simply using the hands as a medium.

But for most of us, palmistry is a bit like reading and writing. You must learn the basics before you tackle Shakespeare or set out to write your own literary masterpiece.

Once the basics are learned, reading palms is like an exciting journey, and I remain enthusiastic about its potential to enlighten people. But I'm also very cautious, and so should you be. Much harm has been done by some practitioners of palmistry out of greed and self-importance. All too often, people become involved with palmists and others in the occult arts at a time when they're deeply disturbed and therefore vulnerable to charlatanism.

*The Line of Fate is discussed in detail in Chapter Six and the Appendix.

I met a woman who paid a palmist $60 to burn candles for her after being told by the reader that enemies were undermining her life. The candles were to ward off their "evil influence." Frightened people have told me of palmists who have told them they're going to die young, have a tragic accident or lose one of their children. I would not hesitate to beat it out the door of any reader who began disclosing such nonsense.

The palm will *not* tell you the length of your life. Rather, it will indicate the *quality* of life you're going to lead or have led—whether or not you're living a robust, involved life or one of mere existence. It can indicate tragedy that may occur if you don't heed the signs of events that can detract from the rich, full experiences available to you. We are all both good and bad, and it shows in the hand. It is up to us to select which parts of us we want to develop.

Palmistry, in itself, falls into that genre considered the "occult sciences." And that doesn't bother me, even though I tend to be cynical. I would rather have it outside the realm that invented the bomb.

I believe a good healthy dose of cynicism is important when you are investigating anything that pertains to your spiritual enlightenment. If we displayed even a little bit of cynicism, greedy TV evangelists wouldn't be fleecing their flocks of millions; and individuals wouldn't pay thousands of dollars to some charlatan for "psychic" cancer, diabetes or arthritis cures. Nor would we buy into the latest diet fad.

My cynicism comes naturally. I was a reporter for eight years, specializing in health and psychology. During that time I also covered police beats and dealt with politicians, con artists and murderers. I also interviewed dozens of people involved in the occult sciences, from those who practiced "aurvoyance" (aura-reading) to handwriting experts.

I've witnessed the stunned looks of hard-edged detectives working on a murder case when a leading California psychic, Dixie Yeterian, led them on a trail in mountainous terrain to uncover a missing piece of evidence and was able to describe the killer to an artist (the sketch was sent over the wires to other police departments).

And I was once sued for $2 million for printing the truth about a cancer quack who made a fortune bilking thousands of dollars from suffering cancer victims. The suit was dropped when it was shown that I had documents and other evidence to back up everything I had written. All of his "patients" eventually died of cancer, probably hastened by his treatments, and he was eventually sent to prison.

To this end, I appreciate the work of other cynics such as Paul Kurtz, a paranormal investigator and chairman of the Committee for the Scientific Investigation of Claims of the Paranormal. I may not agree with his entire philosophy (he's really a hardnose), but we need people like him to keep us in touch with reality.

Therefore, when I'm asked if I really "believe" in what I'm doing with palm-reading, I can give a qualified "Yes, because I believe in possibilities."

Because of my reasoning, I've never turned palm-reading into a business. That is, I have never charged for a reading, but have dealt with it much as a curious researcher. I've had the pleasure of studying hundreds of palms in person, from prints and pictures, and have found some of the findings amazing. I've also published several magazine articles on the subject.

I've seen the proof of some aspects of palmistry and it's brought joy into my life. I've also seen some pretty shabby things said and done in the guise of palm-reading and I'm turned off by those who try to set themselves up as seers with all of life's answers.

Life is tough and people need all the extra possibilities they can grasp. On the other hand, what is good news to one person may not be to another.

I once told a thirty-six-year-old mother of two teens that when she was about forty-three years old, she would have another child. When she became pregnant at age forty-two, she kidded me about how it was all my fault. To her, getting pregnant at that age was OK. To me, already the mother of three at the time, it would have been devastating.

I can't tell people how long their lives will be, but based on the shape and color of their hands, from the lines and mounts, and by comparing those markings, I can tell them the quality of the life they're capable of leading, and I can point out the roadblocks.

Then it's up to them to take the appropriate action.

If a person's hand shows more than one marriage, I can show them other formations that indicate life will go on, but down different roads than they had planned to take. I can also warn them if it looks as if they're heading for a dangerous fork in the road. The choice to do something about it is up to them.

You might ask, "But what can I do about it if that's the way I am?"

Plenty! As a person changes, so do the lines on their hands, regardless of the formations they were born with or may have acquired as they have aged.

Our hands are frequently similar to those of our parents, and the left hand of a right-handed person (and vice versa) gives us clues to our past. It also reveals inherited characteristics.

It was once believed that children's environments accounted for most of their personality traits, but scientific studies now indicate that up to fifty percent of a child's temperament may be inherited.

For this reason, *the right and left hands should both be studied and compared.* On a right-handed individual, if the left hand shows stronger, more meaningful characteristics than the right, it can signify that the person isn't making the most of their inherited capabilities; or you might find that the person has achieved far more than the left hand portends.

Although the scientific community has long scoffed at palm-reading, during the past few years they've been taking a new look at the information contained therein regarding physical and mental health.

Stanley Coren of the Department of Psychology, University of British Columbia, Canada, stated in *The Bulletin of the Psychonomic Society* in 1987 that "There is a good deal of evidence from twin and family studies that dermal ridge patterns are strongly determined by genetic factors. The usefulness of these dermal patterns as indicators of genetically based syndromes has been shown in relationship to a number of disorders known to be due to chromosomal or genetic sources." These ridge-pattern studies on the fingers and palms are called "dermatoglyphics" by the scientific community.

In a paper by anthropologist Cheryl S. Jamison of Indiana University presented at the Association of Physical Anthropologists in 1987, she stated that the learning disability dyslexia can be determined at an early age by a study of ridge patterns on the palm.

They are also being used to identify predispositions to other central-nervous-system irregularities such as stuttering, migraine headaches, auto-immune disease, left-handedness and mathematical giftedness.

Jamison states in her paper that the development of the telltale ridge patterns occur (based on several other studies) when prenatal testosterone is circulating in both male and female fetuses during the period of dermal ridge formation.

Male fetuses begin producing testosterone at approximately 10 gestational weeks and females by about 13 weeks, although females typically produce a far smaller amount. Since dermal ridge formation occurs between the 12th and 19th gestational weeks, there is more than adequate time for the presence of this steroid in the circulation of both sexes to affect their ridge development.

It has long been my belief that the development of certain lines and formations take place during gestation, and that many of these characteristics are inherited (genetic).

I have no quarrel with those in the mental and physical health community who claim that the major lines of the palm are formed by the way we hold our hands. It's all part of our body physiology and gives us clues to our behavior. If a person holds their shoulders continually in a taut position, it tells you that the person is uptight. Likewise, if the hands are held in a rigid position for any length of time, the fingers, mounts, lines and shape of the hand itself are going to form accordingly.

This is similar to a piece of paper that is folded or crumpled. It's certainly bound to leave traces of those folds when it's flattened again. Therefore, if a person tends to hold their hands in a position that increases the depth or length of one of the major lines, that line tells us something about the character of that person.

The position in which the hands have been held, which causes some of these formations, plus the creation of certain lines during gestaton, give credibility to the uniqueness of everyone's hands. Palmistry simply explains what those formations might portend, and in the years ahead, the scientific study of dermatoglypics should add new insights into the study of the hands.

The medical community, too, is taking a new look at the hands. Studies at the University of Florida College of Medicine indicates that eye and kidney diseases brought about by juvenile diabetes can be detected by checking the fingers.

Richard V. Lee, M.D., a professor of medicine at the State University of New York at Buffalo, has said that the nails of the hand provide clues about circulation, heart and lung disease, nutrition, arthritis and many other diseases.

Dr. James Miller of the Children's Hospital in Vancouver, Canada, says many chromosomal disorders in children can be indicated by fingerprint patterns; and Dr. Mark H. Swartz of Mt. Sinai Medical Center in New York has said that fingertip patterns give clues to some heart conditions.

Other research on dermal ridge formations has linked them to schizophrenia. In a report from *Psychiatric News*, R. Srinivasa Murthy, M.D., associate professor of psychiatry at the National Institute of Mental Health and Neurosciences in Bangalore, India, states that specific palmprint patterns have been found in the hands of schizophrenic individuals.

In light of these and other recent findings, *The Journal of the American Medical Association* has stated, "The human hand is a unique organ from which an extraordinary amount of clinical information may be derived."

But palmistry is not new to the world of medicine. In the middle ages palmistry was included in the curriculum of medical faculties. Palmists have been ahead of doctors in this area for generations, but have carried it further. If the hand gives us so much information about our mental and physical health, why not our potential and desires? Aren't they all interconnected?

Certainly during the last decade, the scientific community has come to terms with the mind-body connection. Barrie Cassileth, psychologist and medical sociologist at the University of Pennsylvania Cancer Center, summed it up by saying in *Science Digest*, "No one questions that emotions and health are related."

Norman Cousins says in *Anatomy of an Illness* that biochemical manifestations of mental powers are well documented. He mentions the yogis in India who are able to slow down their pulse to a few beats per minute, or whose skin can be made to resist burning hot surfaces.

The mind-body connection also gives man more control of his own life and destiny, which has been much overlooked in the ancient writings on palmistry that held a more fatalistic view of life. Thus, many people in India believed they were "fated" to live within a certain class, but had hopes of being born into a higher "caste" during another lifetime. So they were complacent in accepting their lot in this life.

Modern-day palmists may or may not believe in reincarnation, but they aren't complacent in acceptig an unrewarding life for anyone. That's why palmistry's major role isn't in divinaton, but in uncovering a person's hidden potential as shown in the hands.

Because technology has outpaced the development of our philosophies—we've become involved with nuclear power before we know how to dispose of the waste, as an example—men and women are beginning to turn inward for some of the answers to the long-neglected aesthetics of life. They want to tap into the self.

"What can I contribute, and how can I exist with purpose during my sojourn on earth?" have now become important questions.

Palmistry is one of the tools that can be used to help answer some of these questions. Although it is based on an ancient tradition, its basic elements are as viable today as in any time throughout history.

Palmistry's origins appear to spring from the ancients of India; from there it spread throughout the world, picking up the flavors of various countries that have adapted it to their own cultures. History indicates that the earliest known palmistry was practiced by the Josi caste in the northwest province of India.

It was later practiced in ancient Egypt, Tibet, Persia, China and Greece. Because of the latter country's contact with other parts of the globe, it eventually spread to other peoples.

Palmistry flourished in the old world, but as with many of the mystical sciences, it met with opposition from Christianity and was nearly destroyed, finally seeing some revival in the Middle Ages.

It remained a popular medium in some European and Eastern countries, and was "imported" to the United States through the diverse cultures that eventually made their way to the New World. They brought with them their own cultural preferences for what were considered "good" hands. These proclivities have existed since palmistry's beginnings.

During the dynastic periods in China, emperors were proud of soft hands with extremely long fingernails—a sign that they did no manual work of any sort. Today, soft hands and long fingernails on a man aren't highly esteemed.

As an example of various cultural preferences of the hand, palmists of the 1930s put together a list of preferred hand characters of women, which was reprinted in *The Book of Hands*, by Paul Tabori:

France: Well-proportioned hand, with the palm better developed than the fingers, showing sagacity, intelligence, and a practical common sense coupled with devotion to duty; but also a daring hand, progressive, eager to act and create. The fingers are short and reveal a spirit and heart that always remain young; the hands are eloquent, their gestures clever and expressive, and fingers are conical and well-spaced; a Frenchwoman does good or sins with equal frankness.

Italy: Hands shaped for love, for hate, for jealousy. Vehement and excessive gestures; like the sun of her country, the Italian woman wants to shine and dominate. Her fingers are of mixed shapes, often with slender, skillful and supple hands.

Spain: Childish hands, rather plump, rather greedy and lascivious. Indolent or violent in their gestures according to their frame of mind, Spanish women promise more than they fulfill; they lack a sense of balance.

England: Practical hands; the palm and the fingers are of the same length. The palm is large, the fingers are closely linked. The Englishwoman is worried about everything that concerns her: her health, her love life, her personal and immediate affairs. Her hand seems to dominate the rest of her body but she has not much egotism.

Scandinavia: Shy and modest hands which do not disclose their character; though the gestures are active, they are not revealing; all is held within the mind. But the somewhat austere form hides a vibrant heart and temperament.

Slavs—and especially the Russians: Mysterious hands which remain passive on the surface though the muscles do get agitated underneath. But when such a woman falls in love, her hand becomes caressing, enveloping, or terribly shriveled; it resembles a volcano before an explosion.

Times change, and although we may not try to determine the ideal hand of an American woman, we still want to know about the things that concern us during our particular lifetimes.

Because I am concerned about the nuclear arms race, I'm continually looking at the hands of children to see if their palms show any indication of turmoil and devastation. Fortunately, their palms show as much life in them as do those of the older generation. This eases my mind somewhat about the possibilities of a nuclear holocaust—at least for now.

But palm-reading is not all seriousness. It has its lighter side.

Once, early in my avocation, when I had agreed to dress up as a gypsy (which is tough, since I'm about five feet, nine inches tall and have reddish hair and a fair complexion) to give brief readings at my children's school Halloween carnival, I told the PTA president that she had two Marriage Lines on her hand.

She immediately ran to her husband, who happened to be her first one, and told him. He crowded in front of the line of children, yelled some obscenities at me and let me know a few of his own ideas on the art of palm-reading.

My thought was that perhaps shooting him would be quicker than a divorce. However, she waited two years for the divorce, and then the terrible truth came out that he had beaten her throughout their marriage.

Another time, while reading the hand of a thirty-five-year-old bachelor, I told him that he was a bit tied to his mother's apron strings. The lady of whom I spoke appeared in the room and loudly announced that they used to burn people like me at the stake.

So, while I take my palmistry seriously, I don't try to elevate it to the role of my answer machine of life. I do believe we can learn from what the palms have to tell us. Palmistry can enhance life through the insights it gives us, and perhaps lift us out of the doldrums for a space of time.

It is a bit of poetic license that keeps us in touch with ourselves and perhaps binds us more closely to the mystical side of life.

Psychologists Thomas J. Smurthwaite and Roy D. McDonald, writing in *Psychological Reports* in 1987, suggest that people who report mystical experiences show a heightened concern about social problems. This points out my belief that once we're attuned to ourselves and know what we as human beings are all about, we become more caring individuals. We see the interconnections among ourselves.

Unlocking the secrets contained in your hands is a step-by-step procedure that begins with the shapes of the fingers, hands and thumbs and culminates in specific major and minor markings.

When I begin a reading, I first determine whether the subject is right- or left-handed; then I examine and compare both hands at once. After making my comparisons, I concentrate on the hand favored by the person for the more detailed reading (right hand for right-handed people, left hand for left-handed).

Throughout, always bear in mind that one single marking or shape is only a clue. When it is put in context with all the other markings in the hand, then its meaning becomes significant.

We'll begin our journey with the thumb.

CHAPTER ONE

The Thumb

THE THUMB HAS ALWAYS intrigued palmists. Nothing reveals a person's nature more clearly than the shape of the thumb and the way it is held. This places us among the family of primates and is used by anthropologists to determine humanity's ancestral roots.

EVOLUTION OF THE THUMB

We have an opposable thumb—it can move in opposition to the other fingers, which enabled us to manipulate tools during the early stages of our development.

Once out of the trees, we no longer used both our hands and feet to grasp things. Hands became an extended tool, and as they developed, more complex movement became possible. This influenced the entire nervous system, thus speeding up the evolutionary development of the higher portions of the brain.

The thumb has more freedom of movement than the rest of our fingers. As we evolved, it became proportionately larger than that of other primates. This enabled us to grasp smaller objects and manipulate them. Apes can pick up a stick and use it for digging, but they can't whittle it into a spear, or take aim at their prey with much accuracy.

THE POSITION OF THE THUMB

In studying the thumb, notice its position in relation to the rest of the hand, its shape, degree of flexibility, and the three sections of which it is comprised. You could say that a good thumb is worth its weight in gold. Monkeys have tiny little thumbs, which suggests that even if they could carry on a conversation, there would be no real depth to it.

I have a medium-sized, stiff-jointed thumb; it doesn't bend back into an arch easily, although the curve between the thumb and the index finger is quite wide. This stiffness indicates a conservative nature and a rather stubborn disposition. The wide curve between the index finger and the thumb, however, makes me nonjudgmental of people and circumstances (see Fig. 1).

Both Phil Donahue and the late Danny Kaye have wide curves between the index finger and the thumb. People with an ample curve between the index finger and thumb (about 45 to 60 degrees) are more naturally gregarious, confident and possess great self-esteem. They tend to have a more unconventional attitude toward life and are generous in thought and deed. They make friends quite easily.

People whose thumbs are more closely tied to the side of the hand (see Fig. 1), with a smaller curve between the index finger and the thumb (less than 45 degrees), tend to be judgmental. They feel more comfortable around people who share their own beliefs. Nancy Reagan and Tom Selleck have thumbs of this kind.

People with an extreme angle (more than 60 degrees) are excessively flamboyant and often inconsiderate of others.

THUMB LENGTH

Thumb length doesn't have the importance some palmists have given it. It was once believed that the longer the thumb, the higher the intellect. As an example of how this doesn't necessarily ring true, Idi Amin has a fairly long thumb. However, I've noted that Carl Sagan, Kenny Loggins and Katharine Hepburn all have exceptionally long thumbs.

It is simpler and more accurate to observe the general appearance of the thumb—whether it "appears" to be long or unusually short. Most

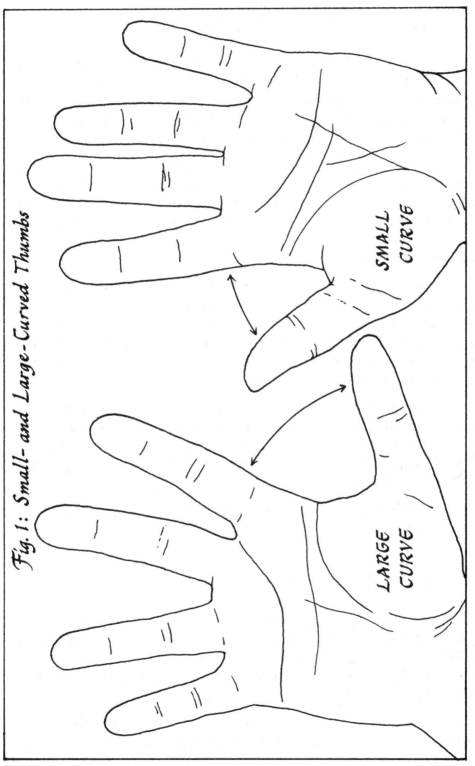

FIG. 1: Large- and Small-Curved Thumbs

thumbs fall somewhere in between. Men, however, tend to have longer thumbs than women, so the two shouldn't be compared.

Women's shorther thumbs once sparked a controversy in West Germany in the mid-'80s. Dr. Karl Juritza had been asked by the Munich Chrsitian Social Union city government to report on the possibility of training women to become fitters, mechanics and electricians.

He testified in court that women weren't physically suited for such work, because among other reasons, they have shorter thumbs than men. He also pointed out that the female body is ten percent shorter than the male's and that women have shorter arms and legs. This made them less efficient, according to the doctor. His testimony cost the women thirty technical apprenticeships that had been made available to them through a government grant.

Why the length of the thumb would make any difference in efficiency is a puzzle to me. I have never noticed that mechanics have exceptionally long thumbs.

The good doctor did point out, however, that women's index fingers tended to be longer than men's. According to palmistry, the index finger (Jupiter) is the finger of authority and leadership.

Women allegedly having longer index fingers is also a puzzle. Long index fingers have long been noted among political and military leaders. Napoleon reportedly had extremely long index fingers—as long as his middle finger. Does this mean that women are better suited to positions of authority?

HIGH- AND LOW-SET THUMBS

A thumb that is set high on the hand will appear to be longer than one that begins farther down the side of the hand.

The high-set thumb usually extends past the first joint of the index finger, whereas the low-set thumb ends nearly at the base of the index finger. The low-set thumb begins closer to the wrist than the high-set one.

It is not possible to simply measure the length of the thumb to determine whether it is short or long. Too much depends on the shape of the hand, which will be covered in Chapter Three. Of course, some types of hands will naturally have longer thumbs.

High-set thumbs indicate a great deal of stubbornness and will-power. These people are usually outgoing, but with bad markings they can be arrogant and bossy.

Low-set thumbs belong to deep thinkers—often philosophers, poets and others given to introspection. With bad markings, however, these people tend to pout and be withdrawn.

EXAMPLES OF HIGH- AND LOW-SET THUMBS

The illustration and prints on the following pages will give you examples of high- and low-set thumbs.

The first print (Fig. 2) is that of Creighton B., a television writer. Like most people with high-set thumbs, he has a dynamic, extroverted personality. Such people like to entertain, and are very open about their feelings.

The second thumb (Fig. 3), which is low set, belongs to Ron R. Low-set thumbs indicate warmhearted people who like to care for others but who often keep their innermost feelings to themselves.

PHALANGES

Phalanges are the narrowing bones that make up the shape of the fingers and are separated by the joints. The thumb is divided into two phalanges. Since the rest of the fingers have three phalanges, some anatomists don't consider the thumbs as fingers.

Palmists divide the thumb into three *sections* (see Fig. 4). The *first section*, or *nail phalange*, stands for will. The *second section/phalange*, below the first joint of the thumb, indicates logic. The *third section* runs into the palm and forms the *Mount of Venus*, which is surrounded by the *Line of Life,** curving out into the palm on the thumb side of the hand. This phalange represents love and the emotional nature of the person.

When the first phalange, representing will, is notably longer than the second, this person relies on willpower to get things done and insists on

---

*The Mount of Venus and the Line of Life will be discussed in detail in Chapters Five and Six respectively.

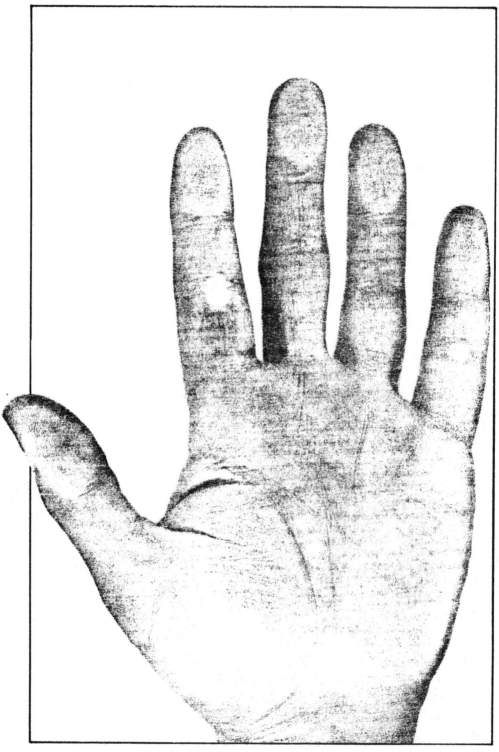

FIG. 2: High-Set Thumb (Creighton B.)

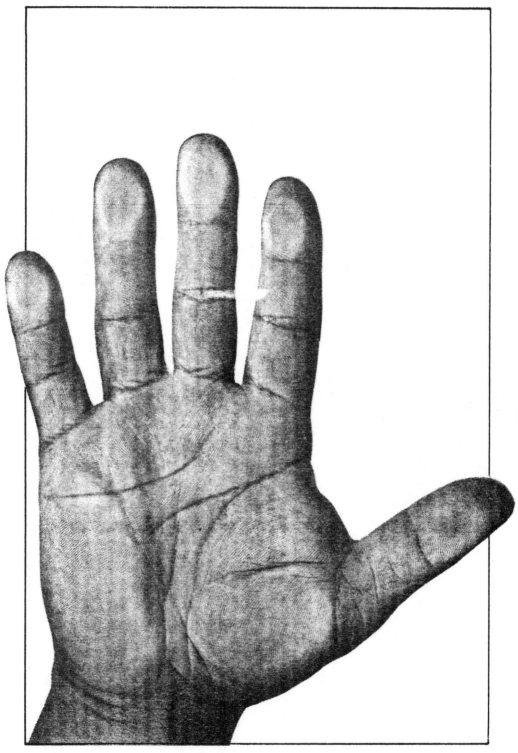

FIG. 3: Low-Set Thumb (Ron R.)

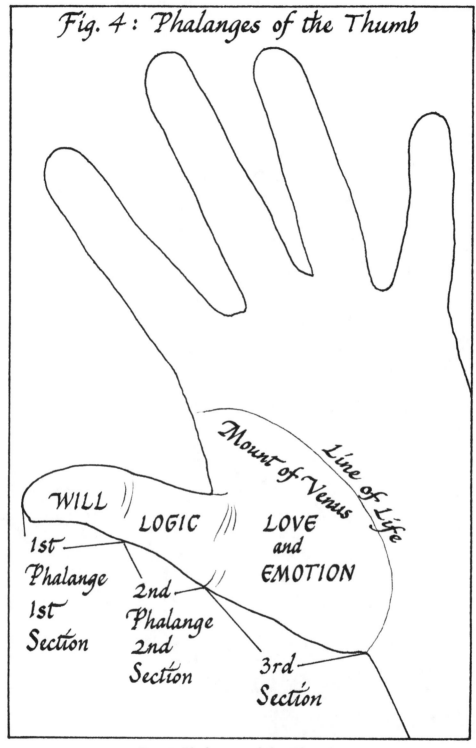

FIG. 4: Phalanges of the Thumb

having their own way. They are slow to change their minds once they reach a decision.

People with well-developed second phalanges, equal in length to or longer than the first (especially if it takes on a waist-like appearance above and below the joint) (see Fig. 5), will use reason and logic to reach their decisions. They make good managers and supervisors because they don't insist on doing things their own way. They are experts at gentle persuasion.

The third section, which embraces the Mount of Venus, is larger than the two phalanges, and makes up part of the palm. If it is excessively large and flabby, coupled with a very small thumb, passion and sensation rules that person's decisions.

SUPPLE- AND FIRM-JOINTED THUMBS

Thumbs that bend backward easily at the first joint between the two phalanges belong to the spendthrifts of life. People with *supple-jointed thumbs* (see Fig. 5) are more extravagant, friendly and outgoing. They will never be lonely and can strike up a conversation wherever they go. They are adaptable and like change. It is as if their thumbs were announcing, "Let me entertain you."

Next time you meet an extremely friendly person who breezes around a room and chats easily with several people, check out their hands and you'll probably find a supple thumb (not to be mistaken for the curve that lies between the index finger and the thumb itself).

The only danger is if this thumb bends too far back and too easily. These people may be glib talkers and have a trunk full of ideas, but they rarely accomplish anything. They can't seem to get started on a project and if they do, rarely complete it. They are impulsive and tend to get involved with members of the opposite sex who frequently take advantage of them.

People with *firm-jointed thumbs* (see Fig. 5) are not as outgoing as their supple-jointed brethren. They do not form friendships easily, but when they do, they make lifelong associations. They are strong-willed problem-solvers who get the job done.

When the thumb is extremely stiff (and there is not much of a curve between the index finger and the thumb), these people want everyone to believe as they do and have trouble understanding those who don't.

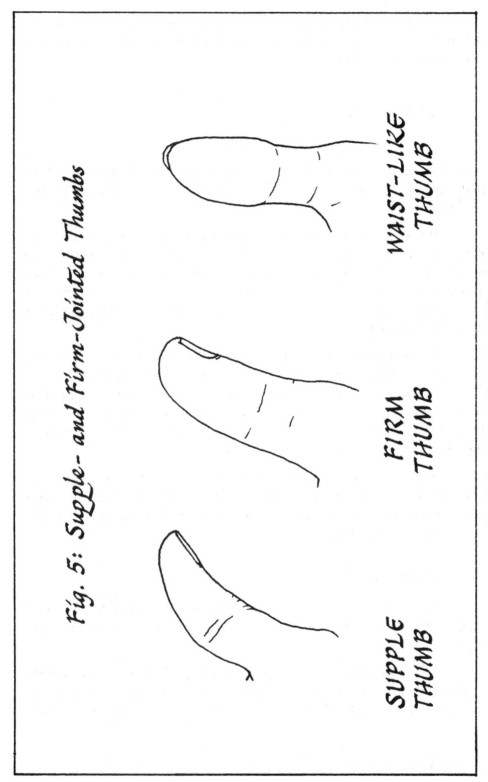

FIG. 5: Supple- and Firm-Jointed Thumbs

People with firm-jointed thumbs tend to be slaves to work and tradition. They suffer more headaches and psychosomatic illnesses than those with supple-jointed thumbs.

THUMB TIPS

The shape of the *thumb tip* has its own meaning. The thumb comes in *square, spatulate* (like a pancake turner), *conic* (slightly pointed), and *clubbed* (bulbous) (see Fig. 6). It has double the meaning of the fingertips.

While *square* fingertips indicate a hard worker who sets about to get the task done immediately, if coupled with a square-tipped thumb, this person can be a real taskmaster. Usually, but not always, a person will have a mixed hand with at least two fingertip types. This prevents them from becoming too rigid in their work patterns and from expecting the same from those around them.*

The *spatulate* thumb belongs to the idea men and women of life. They are inventive and imaginative. This thumb indicates a whirl of activity and thought. Their minds are seldom at rest. Unless the spatulate thumb is modified by the presence of a few square or conic-tipped fingers, their ideas may whip them into a frenzy, but they won't be able to slow their thoughts long enough to get the job done.

A *conic*, or pointed, thumb indicates those who possess a great love of beauty and artistic spirituality. Without the influence of differing fingertips, they become mere observers of the aesthetics of life, doing little in the way of producing anything.

Unfinished Business

Notice the slender tip of the thumb on the following handprint (Fig. 7). This is an example of people who have problems finishing what they start.

A manifestation of the upper phalange, called the *Club Thumb*, which is bulbous in appearance, has long been associated with a violent temper. I have seen this shape on people whom I believe to be very gentle

*See Chapter Two for more on fingertips.

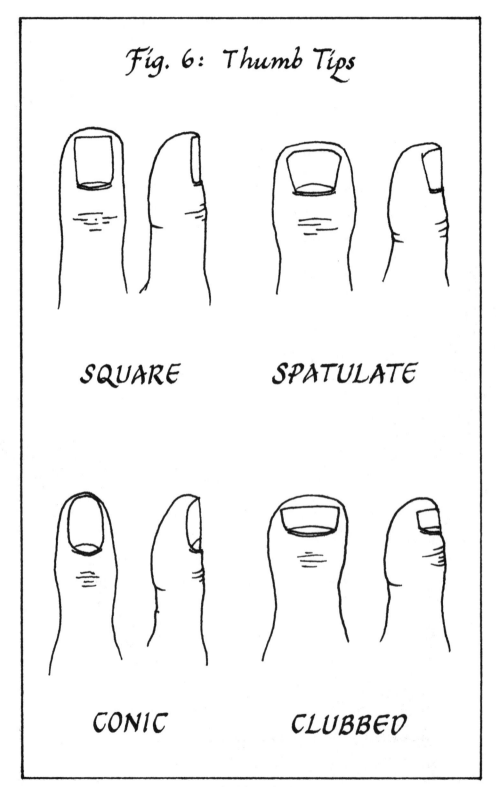

FIG. 6: Thumb Tips

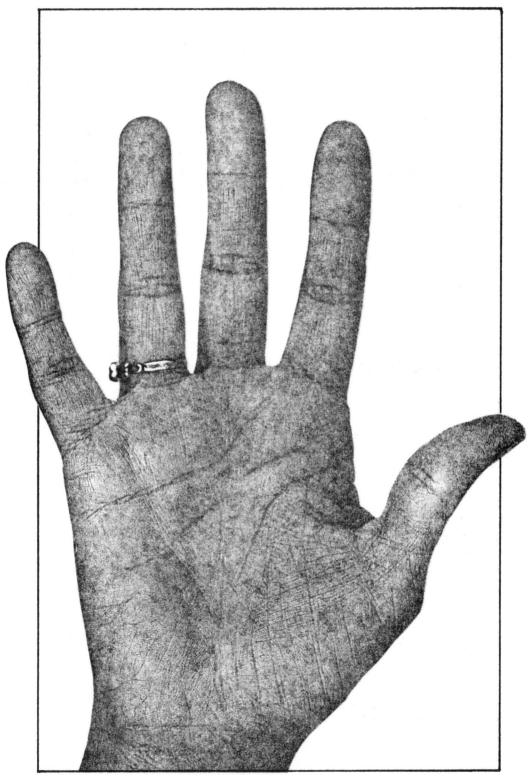

FIG. 7: Unfinished Business (Conic Thumb)

in nature. However, there does seem to be an undercurrent of temper that is rarely displayed, as if lying in wait to be pushed into action.

An example of this might be the clubbed thumb of Spade Cooley, a well-known musician of the '40s and '50s, who died in prison in the 1970s. He received a life sentence for shooting his wife after finding her in bed with another man. From all appearances, Mr. Cooley was a very gentle person.

Here are some qualities associated with various types of thumb tips:

An exceptionally broad, flat thumb indicates a very willful person— a perfectionist who never gives up and always demands their own way.

If the thumb tip is flat (but not excessively broad) when viewed from the side, this person rarely completes projects.

The shorter and thicker the thumb, the more obstinate the person.

CHAPTER TWO

The Fingers

GㅢㅏNCING AT A PERSON'S FINGERS is perhaps the quickest way to size up their personality. The fingers are always on display, and by their size and shape and the way they are held, they reveal many personal traits. You can even look at the hands of politicians waving about on the TV screen and gain some insights into their natures.

LONG AND SHORT FINGERS

Some palmists go so far as to measure the fingers in comparison to the palms to determine if they are *long* or *short*. This can be misleading because certain shapes of hands just naturally have longer fingers. Also, long nails tend to make the fingers appear longer.

When looking at the hand, if the fingers strike you as long in comparison to the shape of the hand, it can be classified as long-fingered, and the reverse for short fingers.

Long fingers may be considered "best" for cosmetic commercials, but beauty is no measuring stick for a person's inner qualities. Both long and short types have outstanding qualities.

Viewed from the nail side, the fingers will appear longer than when seen from the palm side; and in prints taken of a palm, the fingers will appear shorter than they do in real life.

15

Long and short fingers say different things about a person's character. Both can be taken as good signs when the overall shape of the hand is taken into consideration. The length of the fingers takes on the most meaning when they are out of character for the type of hand they are found on—say, extremely long fingers on a square hand.

Long-Fingered Individuals

These people tend to think things through before making decisions. They take their time in selecting a mate, choosing a home or shopping for clothes. Pity the impulsive, short-fingered individuals who are waiting in the car for their long-fingered companions to "pick up a few things."

Long-fingered people are sensitive to details. They include the perfectly dressed executive and the man who looks neat even when he's fixing the plumbing.

Jane Fonda and Barbra Streisand have long fingers. So do Chevy Chase and Johnny Carson.

Long-fingered people, especially if the joints are smooth instead of knotty (which gives the entire finger a waist-like appearance—narrow above and below the joint of the finger), are the type found in the gym every day at the same time, doing precisely what they're supposed to be doing. If they miss a day, it bothers them.

Short-Fingered Individuals

These people abhor routine. They probably won't be bothered at all by missing a day at the gym. After a few sessions they'll probably give it up and try something else anyway.

The short-fingered person is impulsive, has grand ideas and may, with luck, carry some of them through to completion. Dressing to perfection is too much trouble. They tend to be junk-food addicts: whatever fights the hungries is perfectly OK.

Paul Simon, Shirley MacLaine and Cesar Chavez have short fingers.

THE SHAPES OF THE FINGERS

People whose fingers easily *bend backward into an arch* are gregarious and open, possessing magnetic, almost irresistible personalities. However, if they bend too easily,, these individuals lack willpower, are easily influenced by others and are continually asked for favors which they seldom refuse.

People without arching fingers tend to be selective about giving, both of themselves and their possessions.. *Straight-fingered* individuals will still share, but in a cautious manner. Fingers that tend to curve inward, however, are quite selfish in all aspects of their lives.

Thick fingers, especially when short, belong to selfish people.

Raised pads on the insides of the fingertips indicate the person is tactful and sensitive with others.

Puffs near the bottom portion of the fingers indicate self-indulgance. On an otherwise good hand, these puffs can indicate food allergies.

Crooked fingers (other than from the effects of something like arthritis) on a good hand denote a bothersome, irritating person—one always full of senseless questions. Coupled with other bad markings, this crookedness can indicate a crooked nature.

Knotty-jointed fingers (waist-like above and below the joint of the phalanges) belong to gregarious and inquisitive individuals. Mother Teresa has knotty-jointed fingers. Without fail, I've noted that good investigative reporters have them too.

Smooth-jointed fingers are found on people who are more reserved.

Wide spaces between the fingers denote the spendthrifts in life, whether of time, money or in personal habits. Fingers *too close* to one another, however, indicate people who lack zest. They find it very difficult to let go and enjoy themselves.

A *wide space between the little finger and the ring finger* indicates an independent nature, specially if a ring is worn on the little finger.

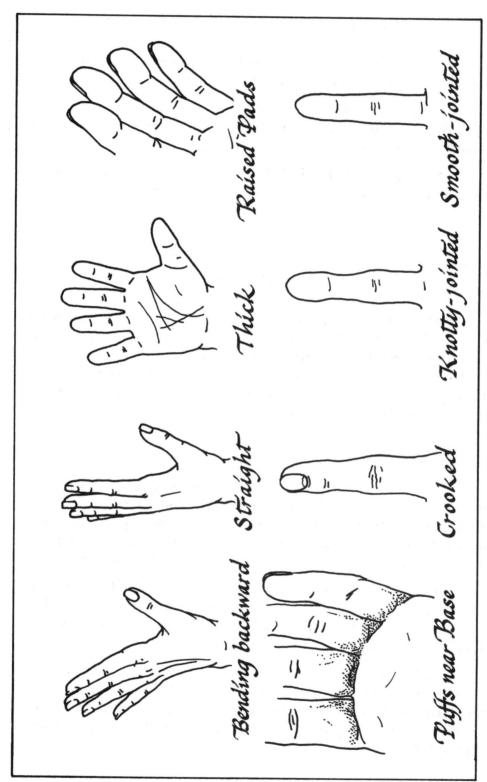

FIG. 8: Finger Shapes

FINGERTIPS

Square fingertips belong to a useful, hardworking, loyal type of person. They are quick to make decisions.

Conic fingertips, which are slightly pointed, are found on all types of hands, but stand for the artistic nature of the person. These people often rely on their intuition to make decisions.

Spatulate fingertips, which flare at the top, grace the hands of creative and impulsive individuals. They are the daredevils of life.

THE INDIVIDUAL FINGERS

Although palmistry's beginnings appear to be in India, it picked up the trappings of the other cultures with which it came in contact as it spread across the globe. The palmistry practiced in European countries, including the United States, has many Greek and Roman influences. The fingers have been given names from these cultures' mythologies and take on the characteristics of the gods so named.

THE LITTLE FINGER

The little finger is called *Mercury* and represents the ability to communicate. Mercury (or Mercurius) is Roman, equivalent to the Greek Hermes, messenger of the gods. In ancient Arab manuscripts, Mercury is a scribe. Hermes is sometimes referred to as the "helpful runner." Hermes is also a bit rambunctious, with a fast and fleeting mind—a glib talker.

His modern-day counterpart, a person with a long little finger, is also gifted in speech. A well-developed little finger makes for a great orator. Many politicians and entertainers have long mercurial fingers. Kenny Rogers and Johnny Carson are among them.

Although shy people tend to have short little fingers, many of them make excellent writers. I've often speculated that Cyrano de Bergerac had short fingers of Mercury, which certainly didn't detract from the beauty of his mind, at least as depicted in the story written by Rostand, the French poet and playwright.

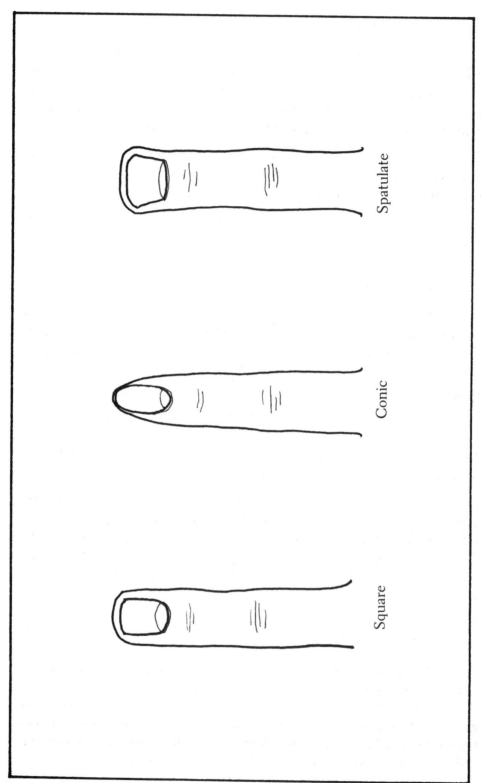

Fig. 9: Fingertips

THE RING FINGER

The ring finger, called *Apollo,* is identified with the Greek sun god. His twin sister, Artemis, became associated with the moon, and both are depicted as warrior types in Greek mythology. Apollo also represents the finger of beauty and the arts. It promises creativity when of good size and is frequently found on the hands of successful artists, musicians and writers.

However, when it is longer than the index finger, it indicates someone who has trouble hanging onto money. Compulsive gamblers have this extra long finger of Apollo.

When the ring finger and index finger are of equal length, the person does well handling personal finances.

THE MIDDLE FINGER

The middle finger is named after *Saturn,* an early Roman agricultural god who later became associated with Kronos, a powerful Greek father god—a judge and ruler. While the names and attributes are largely interchangeable in mythology, in palmistry Saturn is symbolic of "the judge."

A well-balanced Saturn, just slightly longer than the fingers on either side of it, marks a well-balanced person with a keen moral sense. However, when the finger is exceptionally long and quite thick, the person has a melancholy nature and is fond of somber music.

The Romans didn't like to wear rings on the finger of Saturn because they considered it the *digitus infamus* (finger of infamy—bad reputation). To the hand-reader, though, wearing a ring or rings on this middle finger merely signifies a melancholy and often moody person. If the subject wears rings on this digit on both hands, especially if the finger seems thicker than the others, it points up the individual's morbidity.

THE INDEX FINGER

The index finger, known for its link to the god of gods, *Jupiter,* stands for power and authority and the ability to use it correctly. Jupiter is the Roman name for the Greek god Zeus, who certainly loved his power and spread his progeny throughout the world of gods and men at a very rapid rate. In palmistry, a lengthy finger of Jupiter is symbolic of leadership ability, especially when it is longer than Apollo, the ring finger.

The investiture rings of bishops, cardinals and popes are placed on the index finger, the digit of power and authority.

When the finger is nearly as long as or longer than Saturn, it denotes an overbearing nature. These people have leadership ability but tend to overuse it, becoming domineering and excessively aggressive. It can still be a good sign if other markings (which will be discussed in later chapters) are good.

THE RELATIONSHIP OF THE FINGERS

When the ring finger bends toward the middle finger, the person is moody. They also like somber music.

If the index finger bends toward the thumb, the person is not interested in the opinions of others.

Fingers held closely together denote a shy nature.

Fingers placed equally apart from one another indicate a balanced personality.

A little finger that stands away from the ring finger indicates an extremely independent nature. Rings worn on the little finger enhance the person's desire to be independent.

WELL-BALANCED FINGERS WITH STRONG THUMB

The following palm-print (Fig. 10) shows a hand with a strong thumb and fingers which show an excellent relationship among themselves.

THE SHAPES OF THE NAILS

The fingernails are very revealing of a person's mental and physical health. Serious study is being given the hand by some of the nation's top medical research centers and universities. The shape of the nail can indicate whether a person is susceptible to certain illnesses. This doesn't necessarily mean the illness will manifest itself; rather, it is a warning of what to watch for.

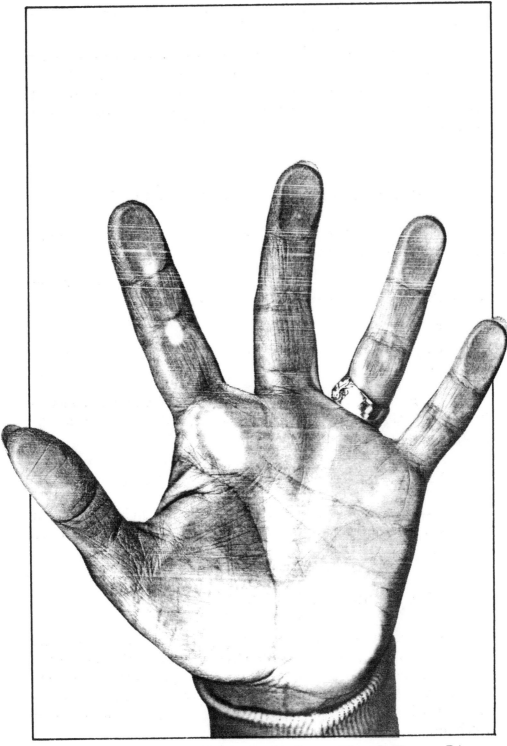

FIG. 10: Well-Balanced Fingers with Strong Thumb (Doreen B.)

Doctors have long observed that most anemics have spoon-shaped nails with a slight hollow in the center. Pitted or frayed nails, split at the ends, occur in psoriasis sufferers. White lines across the nails are a sign of past or present illnesses—as if the illness leaves a marker.

Nails that are long* from base to tip indicate a propensity for chest or lung trouble, especially if the nails curve downward.

Short, small nails indicate a tendency toward heart and cardiovascular diseases.

Small nails that are flat and sunken may be a sign of nerve disease. If they are also brittle and white, loss of movement or paralysis are possible developments.

Brittle nails can indicate a nervous disposition, and when accompanied by extremely dry hands, thyroid problems may be present.

Nails that are wide at the top and appear bluish can mean poor circulation, while extremely thin ones indicate a tendency toward spinal disease.

OTHER FINGERNAIL FACTS

A nervous temperament is shown by flecks or spots on the nails, and this is frequently a sign of stress.

Small, thin nails indicate lack of energy, and when extremely thin and long, lack of zest for life.

Short-nailed individuals tend to be more critical and judgmental, while those with longer nails are more even-tempered.

Short-nailed people generally possess a better sense of humor than long-nailed people.

Red nails indicate high blood pressure.

Bluish nails indicate circulatory problems.

---

*When speaking of long and short nails, I'm referring to the area *within the first phalange,* not that which grows beyond the fingertip.

Meddlesome worry-warts usually have nails that are broader than they are long.

As you might suspect, people who bite their nails have a nervous, worrying disposition. This is often temporary.

I once worked with a woman who normally had long, beautiful nails. But while pursuing her master's degree at a nearby university, she bit her nails until they bled every time finals loomed on the horizon.

CHAPTER THREE

The Shapes of the Hands

The hands may almost be said to speak. Do we not use them to demand, promise, summon, dismiss, threaten, supplicate, express aversion or fear, question and deny? Do we not use them to indicate joy, sorrow, hesitation, confession, penitence, measure, quantity, number and time? Have they not the power to excite and prohibit, to express approval, wonder, shame?

—Marcus Fabius Quintilianus

THE HAND IS A MARVEL to behold. Like a snowflake, there are no two identical hands. There are six basic shapes of hands, but rarely do they exist in their exact forms. All hands are found as mixtures of two or more types. What else could be expected in a culture where artists may also be financial experts and waitresses are philosophers?

THE BEAUTY OF HANDS

Ironically, beautiful hands often lack personality, talent, ambition, courage and care. It took years of reading hands before I learned to appreciate my own, which are less than long and tapering. They are squarish, knotty and short-nailed. So are the hands of artists, business executives, carpenters, interior decorators and philosophers.

The hands of women painted by the masters throughout the Renaissance of the 14th through 16th centuries are depicted as almost bird-like—small and fragile, without mastery of their use. Their subjects were the great ladies and nobility of the day, or idealized conceptions of wood nymphs—unlike the active and diversified women of today.

It took the Impressionists, Realists and Expressionists of later centuries to capture the beauty of the hand in all its forms—delicate, strong, healing, demanding, work-worn, inquisitive, contemplative, questioning, struggling, peaceful and prayerful.

In present-day societies, a useful, purposeful hand is highly regarded on both male and female, just as the graceful hands of the ballerina are. Our hands reveal many things about ourselves.

Few of the most admired women of the past three decades have what could be considered beautiful hands. Jacqueline Kennedy has bold, knotty, large-looking hands, and in her later years she has demonstrated what we suspected all along—that she's a tough, complicated woman. Margaret Thatcher's small hands look like those of a prizefighter's lethal weapons, and she's used them well. As Britain's prime minister, she's been labeled "The Iron Maiden." And the late Indira Gandhi, who once served as Prime Minister of a troubled India, gracefully displayed lengthy, knotty hands that looked as if they could engulf a basketball.

I am prejudiced toward hands that look as if they're contributing something to this troubled world, for the shapes of hands, in all their diversification, are works of art.

Beautiful hands needn't be a drawback. Eleanor Roosevelt had lovely, long-fingered hands as a young women, and they remained graceful into old age.

More often than not, when I begin to read the hands of a woman, she will shyly place her palms in front of me and say, "My hands have always been so ugly." It's as if there's a stigma attached to having strong, capable hands. Women especially have been indoctrinated by TV commercials touting smooth, pampered hands. Such hands are not representative of the majority any more than the film and television sex goddesses are representative of most women. Despite this, women tend to think they lack something if their hands are less than gorgeous.

I've studied men's hands—gnarled, calloused, hardworking—that indicate artistic abilities and deep spirituality. These men seemed just as embarrassed as the women by their calluses, and would frequently say something like, "I don't know if you can see the lines for all the calluses."

Believe me, I can see the lines, and I think it's a pity that we live in a society that doesn't appreciate hands that can build a home or harvest the food for our table.

Alan Alda has gnarled-looking hands. So did Abraham Lincoln.

Men, however, do not appear troubled by feminine, delicate-looking hands. As a matter of fact, they don't seem to notice. An acquaintance of mine, a brilliant man working on his doctorate in English, has such hands. They are long, slender, smooth and quite noticeable on his rather square, stout body. I once remarked to him that his hands didn't match his frame, and he gave me a look of complete incredulity. But a year later, while he was attending the university, my friend told me that one of his English teachers—a sprightly old woman—had also remarked to him that his hands didn't seem to match his body.

I think I've come to appreciate hands in much the same way that an artist or photographer appreciates the lines and formations of a person's face. They show character, and that, in turn, means beauty.

A Square/Philosophic Hand

Dana Brookins, English professor and author of several books, including *Alone in Wolf Hollow*, which earned an Edgar Allan Poe award from the Mystery Writers of America, has hands that look like a Chicago road map on the palm side. Her print is shown on the following page (Fig. 11).

Her hands are a mixture of philosophic and square—the palm itself has a square look to it, but is lengthier than the usual square hand. The multitude of lines indicate someone who will never be bored and never bore anyone else.

As you read through the following chapters, you'll find this an interesting hand to study, and I hope you come back to it after you've mastered some of the major and minor lines. You'll see the inherent talent, the ability to take risks, and financial security after a long struggle.

As an example, Dana's partially square palm means she's a hard worker. Most of the fingers are conic (slightly pointed), which gives her an artistic bent. The curve between the index finger (Jupiter) and the thumb is quite large, making her at ease around people and places of all sorts.

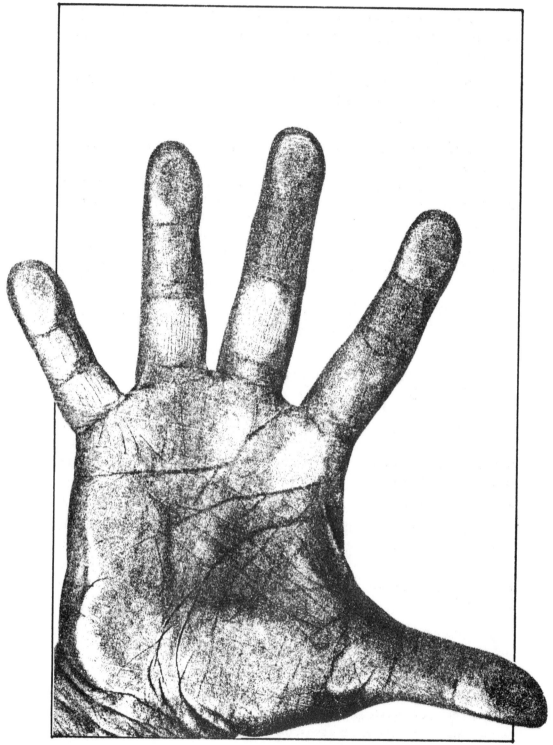

FIG. 11: A Square Philosophic Hand (Dana Brookins)

Palm and finger shapes are the fundamentals of palm reading. This basic information is the foundation for reading the intricacies of the lines and mounts in the palm.

In the preceding two chapters we've studied the shapes of the fingers and thumb. Now we'll proceed to the six basic shapes of the hand and their variations.

Few hands are found with only one pure shape. A palm may be considered square, but the fingers may be conic or spatulate. The thumb, as we've studied in a preceding chapter, may not be square-tipped at all, even though the palm is. This variety of formations makes the person more diversified.

If a hand had a square palm, square fingers, and a square-tipped thumb, this person would be quite frightening. They would literally be "square."

Therefore, when studying the shapes of the hands, all formations— fingers, thumb and palm—must be taken into consideration.

THE SQUARE HAND

The square hand has a palm that is nearly as wide as it is long (see Fig. 12). Often it includes square fingertips and fingers that are quite short. In keeping with the pure square hand, the thumb will be smooth and tied closely to the thumb side of the hand. The curve between the index finger (Jupiter) and the thumb will be narrow.

These people are neat and orderly, lovers of conformity and discipline, make staunch friends, have no great love of poetry or art, tend to be conservative in politics and religion and are sincere and trustworthy in intimate relationships—although they are not demonstrative. They are hard workers.

They have these characteristics because the square look of the palm is reinforced by the other square formations of the fingers and thumb. They are tied to custom and ritual, dogmatism and safety.

They love peace, quiet and harmony, but do not have the ability to work out peaceful settlements in confusing situations; they would tend to shout "quiet," and expect it to happen, and would have difficulty explaining their conservative leanings except to say, "That's just the way it is."

But they are as necessary in a society as their more flamboyant, philosophical, extroverted brothers and sisters with other formations of the hand.

The square hand with spatulate fingers that flare out at the tips is not so tied to conformity as the square hand with square fingers.

These people have inventive minds, which they apply to practical ideas and situations. They love to tinker, but always with a useful purpose in mind. If they are designing a house, it will be functional. They are leaders in energy conservation and time management.

People with spatulate-tipped fingers and square hands prefer getting their exercise by doing something practical, such as gardening or painting the house. Hours spent jogging or at a gym seem a waste of time, although they might enjoy tennis or racquet-ball because they love winning.

The square hand with psychic fingers, so called because it signifies the dreamers of society, is an unusual formation, because psychic hands and fingers are the extreme opposite of square hands and fingers. This is a very rare combination.

The psychic finger is long and pointed, which gives an unusual look to a square palm. Even so, it can be a fortunate formation because it mitigates the extreme conformity of the square hand.

It is beneficial in two ways: it gives the square personality a measure of tenderness and thoughtfulness, and bestows the principles of hard work on an otherwise dreamy nature that all too often shirks the responsibility of hard work.

The square hand with conic fingers is perhaps among the most favorable alliances. Conic fingers are slightly pointed, but not as long as psychic fingers. Conic fingers belong to the artists of the world. Many of our most famous artists and musicians are endowed with at least a few conic fingers.

These individuals possess both the love and talent of the artistic and the discipline and work ethic to accomplish something. They are dreamers, but with practical aspirations. They have no intention of being poor, starving artists.

The square hand with mixed fingers is frequently found in technological societies because they have evolved to contain such diverse peoples. No longer are sons working at the same professions as their fathers, nor living the same type of life as the one they were born into.

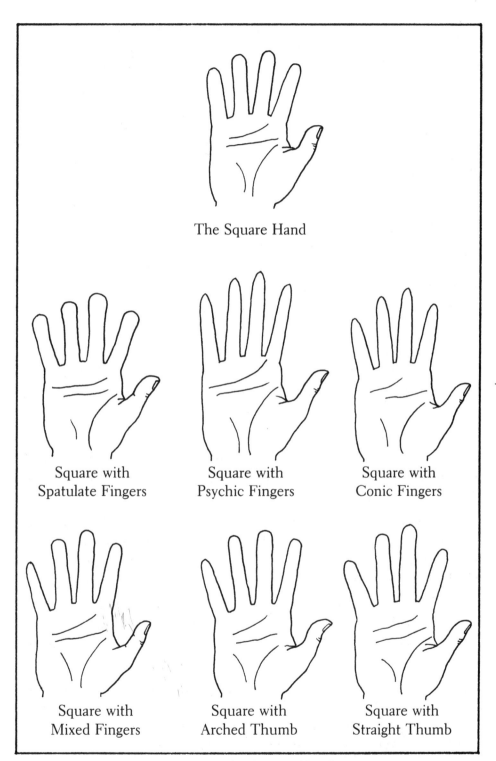

The Square Hand

Square with
Spatulate Fingers

Square with
Psychic Fingers

Square with
Conic Fingers

Square with
Mixed Fingers

Square with
Arched Thumb

Square with
Straight Thumb

FIG. 12: The Square Hand

The square hand with mixed fingers belongs to the computer expert who can also fix the plumbing and who might take up skydiving on the weekend.

Those with mixed fingers—perhaps one conic, another spatulate and two square—are versatile in their everyday lives. With certain other markings (which we'll cover in later chapters), they make great conversationalists because their interests are varied. They may, however, find it difficult to concentrate on one objective and become the proverbial "Jack of all trades and master of none."

The square hand with arched thumb, which bends at the joint between the phalanges, takes away some of the excessive gravity of the totally square-handed person. Although these people may remain conservative, they will carefully weigh other opinions, even if they rarely change their minds. They respect other viewpoints.

The square hand with straight thumb, which doesn't arch at the joint, denotes an extremely stubborn nature. They never change their minds and rarely respect the other person's viewpoint.

A Square Hand with Some Conic Fingers

The following print (Fig. 13) is an example of a square hand with some conic fingers. It belongs to a thirty-eight-year-old Lynette D., a waitress with a degree in interior decorating. The square look of the palm makes her hard-working and quite conservative. The little finger separated from the rest gives her an independent nature.

Other markings on her hand, which you will become acquainted with in following chapters, are also notable, particularly the lengthy Line of Head, running across the center of the palm beneath the fingers. This makes her quite intelligent. You may want to return to this print when studying the Line of Head (see Chapter Six).

The hand has a good thumb, balanced between will and logic. She will stick to the decisions she makes.

THE SPATULATE HAND

The spatulate hand resembles the square hand, but is *broader* either at the *wrist* or at the *base of the fingers*, giving it the shape of a spatula (see Figs. 14 and 15).

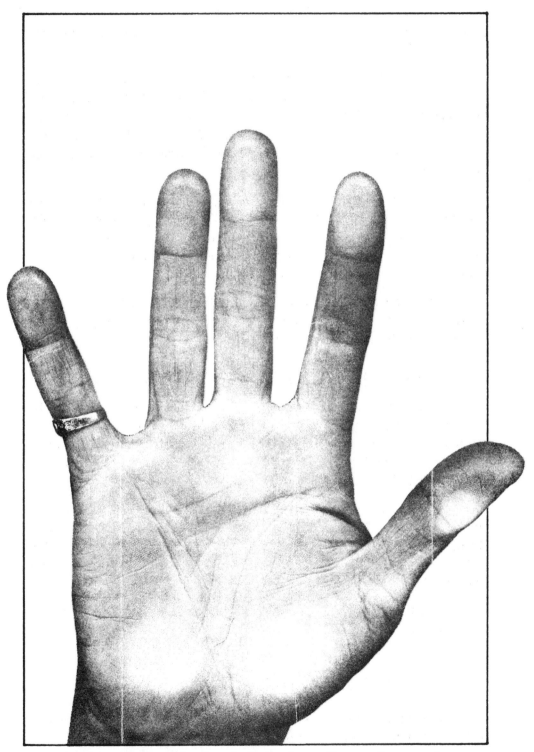

FIG. 13: A Square Hand with Some Conic Fingers (Lynette D.)

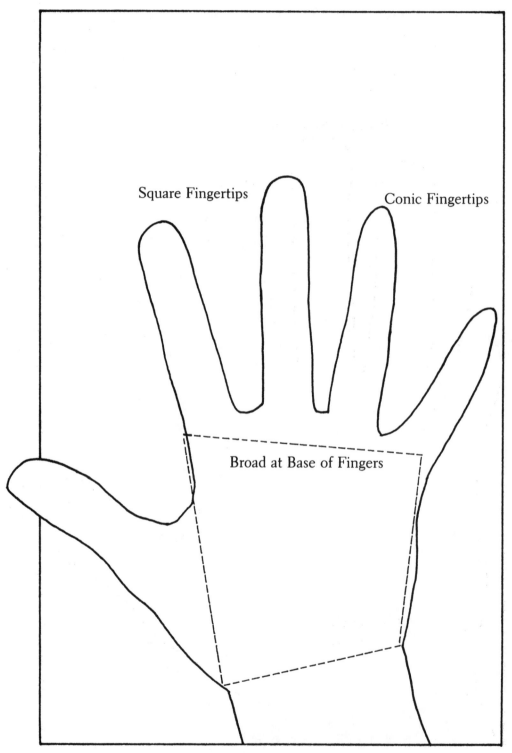

Square Fingertips

Conic Fingertips

Broad at Base of Fingers

FIG. 14: The Spatulate Hand, Variation I

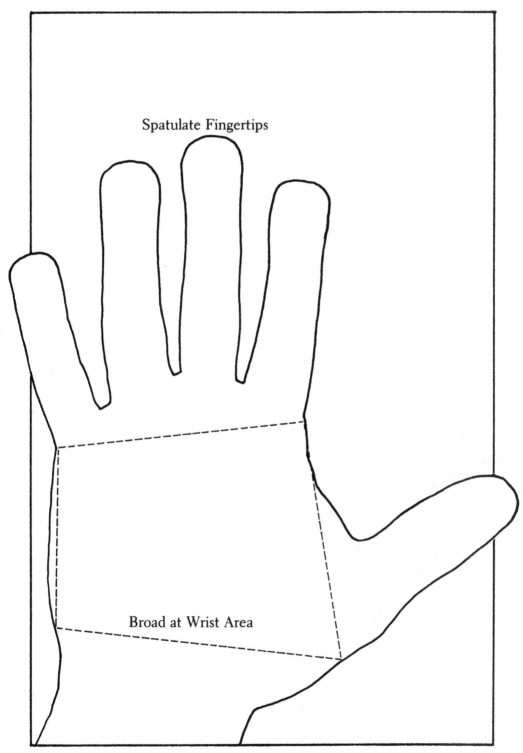

Spatulate Fingertips

Broad at Wrist Area

FIG. 15: The Spatulate Hand, Variation II

While the hand may appear to be clumsy, the mind behind the hand can be the cleverest of all if other manifestations are present. People with this hand are full of energy, action, independence and ideas. They are the inventors—the New Wave people among us. They love challenge and are original with their ideas. They are often misunderstood because of their preoccupation with problem-solving. They always have a better way of doing things, and even though they are frequently correct, they often alienate those who prefer the safer roads of life.

If the broad development is at the base of the fingers, they are practical in their inventiveness. When the broad part is near the wrist, the ideas aren't as practical.

A soft, spongy, spatulate hand means that the person is restless by nature but lacks the discipline to accomplish goals.

The spatulate hand with square fingers, that is, fingers that are rather blunted, might detract a bit from the inventiveness of a person with a spatulate-shaped palm, but they will always find uses for their creativity. Their ideas may not be as inspired as those of people with conic and spatulate fingertips, but because they are such hard workers and stick to the tasks at hand, they will follow through on them.

When asked to design a new product for a specific use, they will work diligently to produce it, whereas the person with spatulate hands and spatulate-shaped fingertips will often come up with something altogether different—useful, but not what the boss wanted.

The spatulate hand with spatulate fingers is the true dreamer, the inventor who makes his work his life. Ideas abound, and the mind is always clicking. Their owners struggle with ordinary, day-to-day living; they just don't have time for routine.

If they're lucky, and have other good markings on the hand—strong lines to indicate mental acuity, and firm, elastic palms—they stand a chance of making their names known. If other formations indicate laziness and lack of discipline, they may remain unfulfilled dreamers.

The spatulate hand with conic fingers, which have more delicate, rounded fingertips, may seem out of character. Spatulate hands are usually strong and vibrant-looking, whereas conic fingertips appear gentle.

Conic fingertips add an artistic flare to the spatulate, and a love of beauty and luxury. Because the energy of the spatulate hand is combined with the more indolent conic, these people are continually at odds with themselves. They want to create, and the energy abounds, but they have a lazy streak that they're continually resisting. They often manage, through sheer willpower, to become noted artists or inventors.

A SPATULATE HAND

The following spatulate-shaped hand (Fig. 16) belongs to Paula D., an office manager for a large group of psychiatrists, who does free-lance bookkeeping on the side. Spatulate-shaped hands belong to people with a flare for independence.

Married at sixteen and divorced in her early twenties, Paula is the mother of a teenager. Following her divorce she put herself through college and then moved from her hometown in Pennsylvania to California, where her career began.

THE CONIC HAND

The conic hand, often called the artistic hand, is of medium length with tapering, medium-length palm and rounded fingertips (see Fig. 17). It is a graceful-looking hand but has many variations, which can make for either greatness or indolence. The conic type has as its roots restlessness, impulsiveness and a love of luxury.

Leonardo da Vinci's *Mona Lisa* has conic hands, although the palms show more strength than is usually found in purely conic hands.

The conic hand in its pure form, with conic-shaped palm and fingertips, provides the artistic temperament, but these people lack the discipline and stamina required to become successful painters, writers, actors or other artistic types. Many people with conic hands, although not artists in their own right, surround themselves with artistic people, often as benefactors.

Conic-handed people are emotional and easily influenced by the people around them.

The conic hand with square-tipped fingers, which add a look of strength to the hand, promotes the discipline and stamina required for artistic success. Without this tempering of at least some of the fingertips, a

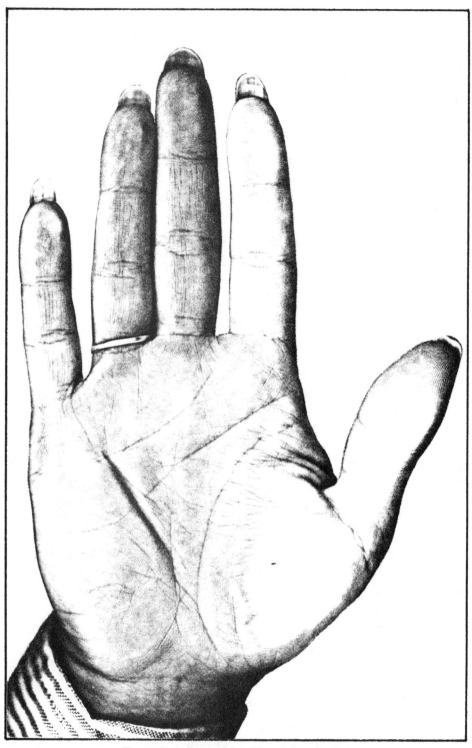

FIG. 16: A Spatulate Hand (Paula D.)

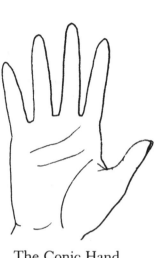

The Conic Hand

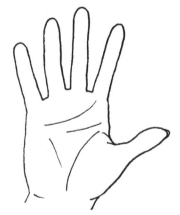

The Conic Hand
with Square-Tipped
Fingers

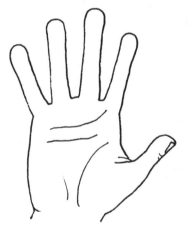

The Conic Hand
with Spatulate-
Tipped Fingers

FIG. 17: The Conic Hand

firm elastic palm or other favorable markings, conic-handed people seldom achieve anything of lasting artistic value.

Leo Buscaglia, the columnist who promotes love, has conic hands with square-tipped fingers.

A Conic Hand with Some Square-Tipped Fingers

The palm-print shown on the following page (Fig. 18) is of a conic hand with some square-tipped fingers and belongs to a thirty-eight-year-old copy editor of a Los Angeles area newspaper. Were it not for the square-tipped fingers, Barbara T. would be in trouble because her hands show that love of luxury and indolence associated with purely conic hands.

True to the nature of conic-handed people, Barbara's interest in the theatre, art and literature is fervent. Her house is decorated to perfection and she dresses with class.

You may want to check this hand again when you get into the chapters on fingers and major lines. You'll note that her little finger (Mercury) stands apart from the rest of her fingers, which is an indication of an independent nature. This is emphasized by the ring she wears on that finger.

Note the short Line of Head (the second line down that runs beneath the fingers of the palm: this indicates a materialistic nature. It nearly bumps into a second Line of Head (an unusual formation) that is going in a different direction. The second Line of Head is the antimaterialistic, antiestablishment, '60s-flower-child side of her nature. This double nature will always cause confusion in her life.

The conic hand with spatulate-tipped fingers belongs to the innovators of the artistic world. These are the people who dare to be different in dress and home decoration and who set their own style of entertaining. They are fun people to be around but demand center stage.

THE PHILOSOPHIC HAND

The philosophic hand is an entity unto itself (see Fig. 19). It usually doesn't combine with square, conic or spatulate fingers.* The palm is

*However, refer back to Fig. 11 for an exception.

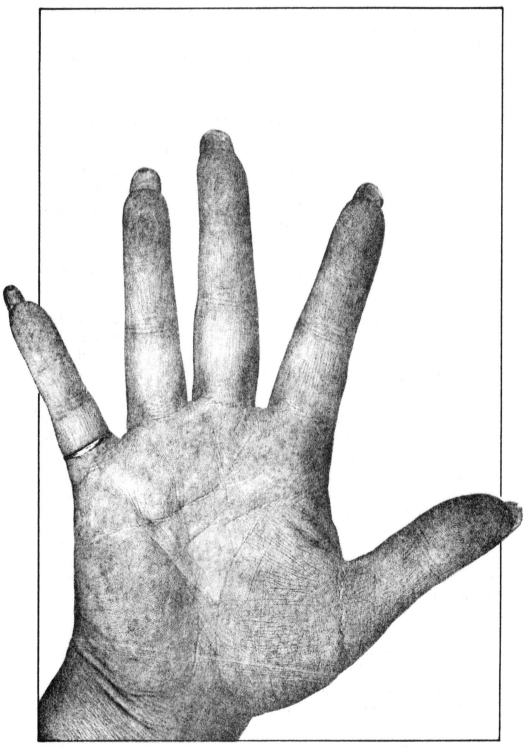

FIG. 18: A Conic Hand with Some Square-Tipped Fingers (Barbara T.)

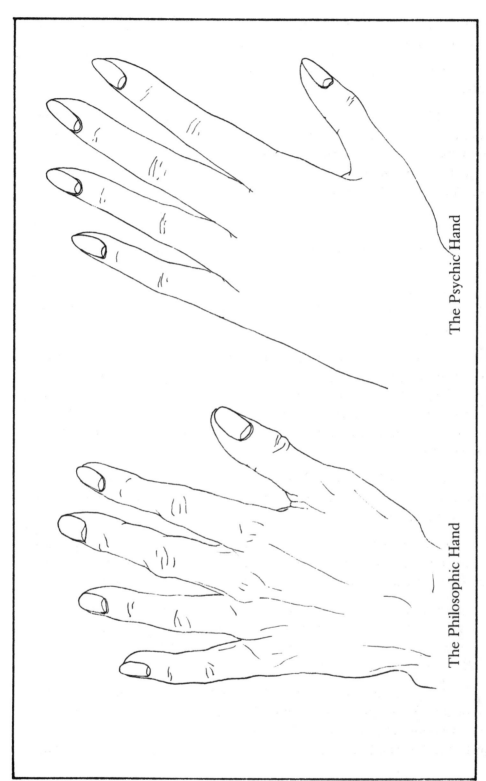

The Psychic Hand

The Philosophic Hand

FIG. 19: The Philosophic & Psychic Hands

lengthy and angular with bony fingers and developed joints. The hand looks inquisitive and the palm is often covered with a multitude of lines.

The fingertips tend to be pointed but can't be classified as conic because of the developed joints.

Philosophic hands belong to philosophers, futurists, Jesuits, nuns and those who live a contemplative life with a vision. These hands are most often found in Eastern countries, especially among mystics. Liberal theologians tend to come closer to having philosophic hands than do conservative Christian leaders, whose hands are usually square.

THE PSYCHIC HAND

The psychic hand, like the philosophic, is usually not mixed with other finger types (see Fig. 19). Its name has nothing to do with the term "psychic" as we know it today.

It is one of the most beautiful and yet most unfortunate of hand shapes. It is fragile-looking, with thin palm, long, tapering fingers and almond-shaped nails. Owners of these hands are used to people's flattering remarks about the beauty of their hands. The flattery usually ends there, however, for those with psychic hands have a tough time finding their place in Western society.

They avoid the hustle and bustle and are trusting, gentle, compassionate and idealistic. Surprisingly, owners of these hands, if other markings are good, are full of hidden strengths.

Children with psychic hands, if they are the offspring of caring, understanding parents, will be channeled into endeavors where they can thrive. If the parents are harsh, these children will wither and die.

Psychic-handed people can be creative, charming and intelligent, especially if they find occupations to suit them. They should, however, have business people take care of their finances and have someone to remind them of appointments.

They are sensitive to the needs of others and are often found in the mystic arts as mediums, clairvoyants, Tarot-card readers and in related occult vocations. They are counted among the New Age philosophers, therapists and healers, but they usually don't have pure psychic hands. The pointed fingers give way to a square look. This helps give them the stamina to deal effectively with life. They do, however, retain their sensitivity.

AN EXAMPLE OF A PSYCHIC HAND

The following example of a psychic hand (Fig. 20) belongs to Liz T., a university professor. Although the palm is psychic-shaped, some of the fingers are square. This adds strength to the hand.

She tends to be judgmental of others, as shown by the thumb that seems tied to the side of the hand, but this is tempered by her sensitivity. She will go out of her way not to hurt anyone but still can't understand why people do the silly things they do.

THE MIXED HAND

The mixed hand is impossible to put into any one category. It looks like it might be square, and then again, perhaps spatulate. The fingers come in a variety of shapes—sometimes conic, but usually square and spatulate. Its owner will be adept at a variety of jobs.

They are multi-faceted people and are much neglected in many societies. They love children, but don't want to be tied down to them. They can love deeply, but feel hemmed in by the prospects of being married to one person for life. They can be hard workers, but don't like routine.

People with mixed hands may have a multitude of talents, depending on other markings, but they find it difficult to finish one project. They jump from one thing to another but add sparkle wherever they go.

AN EXAMPLE OF A MIXED HAND

The following (Fig. 21) is an example of a mixed hand, but one of ideas rather than material trappings. Its shape can't be categorized. The hand belongs to Leslie E., a metaphysical counselor who lives in the mountain community of Wrightwood in California.

He is a natural teacher of metaphysics, as shown by the Ring of Solomon, that small arched line lying beneath the index finger, and the lengthy Line of Head, which travels across the palm and goes off the side of the hand.

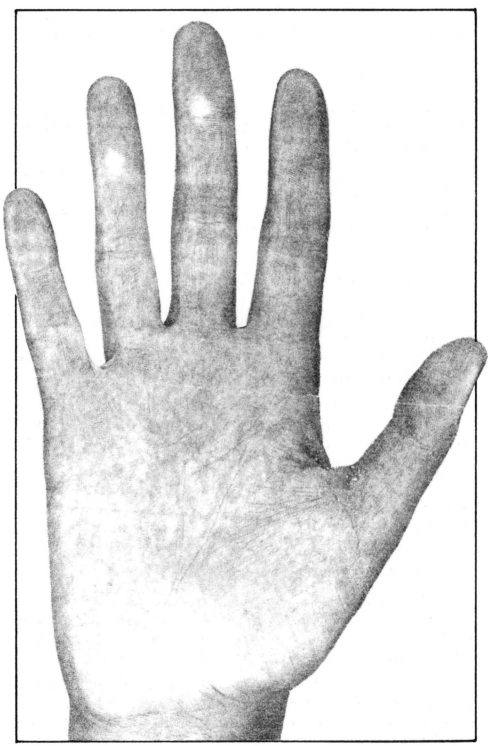

FIG. 20: The Psychic Hand (Liz T.)

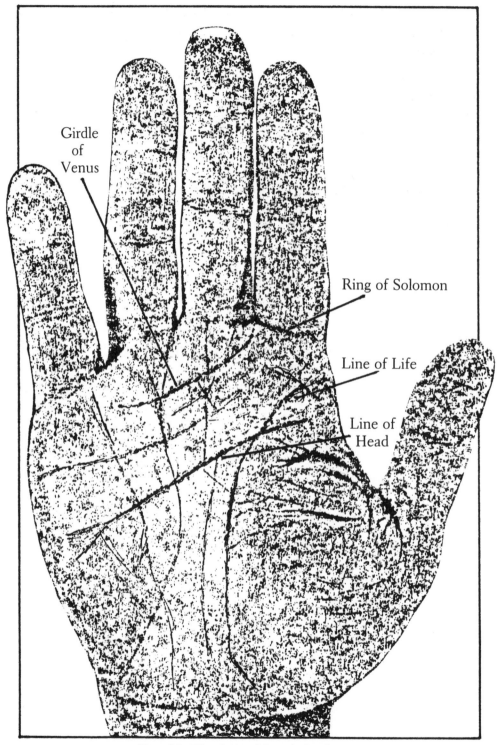

Girdle of Venus

Ring of Solomon

Line of Life

Line of Head

Fig. 21: The Mixed hand (Leslie E.)

The Line of Head gives him great intelligence, but because it is tied to the Line of Life, which circles the thumb on the palm, he is afraid to take chances.*

Leslie's hand also contains a Girdle of Venus, the faint line running beneath the fingers between the index and middle fingers. People with this marking are highly sensitive but moody and touchy about little things. They are easily offended.

*The various lines of the hand will be explained in detail in Chapters Six and Seven.

CHAPTER FOUR

Hand Language

Many aspects of a person's character are revealed simply by the way they hold their hands and fingers. Palmists frequently size people up by the way they hold their hands long before they glance at the palm itself for a complete reading.

Also, it's fun to watch the hands of politicians on TV or in public to get an idea of their worth before they ever begin their speeches.

Dr. Charlotte Wolff, in *A Psychology of Gesture*, says that "the whole body can participate in the language of gesture, whilst verbal language is restricted to the organs of speech." She further states that "Emotions are freed by unrestricted movements. They become inhibited and atrophied by suppression of gesture."

HAND MOVEMENTS

The movement of our hands affects our very being—how we view the world, our work, friends and acquaintances. Even our religious manifestations show in hand movements. Raised hands, with palms showing outward, indicate salutation, worship or surrender. Civilizations that turned to the heavens for their gods turned their palm upward in supplication. Civilizations that worshipped earth gods represented in trees, stones, water and growth turned palms downward in worship.

Hand movement is a language of its own and one to which we generally pay little attention. But therapists pay attention to the hands. A marriage and family counselor once told me that people who place their hands between their crossed knees have problems with their sexuality.

During a seminar on "The Healing Power of Laughter and Play," which I covered for a newspaper, I learned how body movements, including the hands, affect our moods. Matt Weinstein, health professional and president of Playfair Inc., demonstrated through audience participation how the body can be at odds with the brain when it says it's depression time.

If you jerk your arms upward and clap your hands while shouting enthusiastically, "I'm depressed," you'll get the giggles and soon the depression will go away.

I've used this exercise from time to time when I've been in the pits. It puts me back on track. At first it's an effort to raise my drooping, lifeless hands upward, but by the second try, my entire mood has changed.

Some hand movements are not as obvious. But as you become acquainted with these gestures, you'll automatically make mental notes of the people who use them.

The first thing to notice is whether the hands are generally spread open or clenched. If the fingers tend to show spaces between them in a relaxed position, the person is open-minded. When clenched, narrow-minded.

When the thumb is tucked into the fist, the person has a guilt complex or is trying to hide some event in their past.

When the ring finger (Apollo) and the little finger (Mercury) are bent downward toward the palm, it is a sign of someone who is afraid to speak out at the moment.

Washing hands is a ritual of innocence.

Rubbing the palms together can mean cunning.

If the fingers are held tightly together, the person feels inhibited.

When the thumb looks tense, stiff or tied down to the hand, the person is feeling intimidated.

If the ring finger bends into the palm by itself, the person is purposefully withholding information.

Hands clasped together with the fingers entwined is a sign of someone contemplating their next move, especially when the fingers are held beneath the chin.

When the hands are placed together without the fingers entwining, but with the thumbs wrapped around each other, the person is waiting for your next move.

If the hand is clenched and the thumb is pressed against the lips, the person is contemplating their own next move.

The hand placed on the breast signifies an attitude of knowledge.

The circle formed by touching the thumb and forefinger is a sign of approval and perfection in many cultures.

Placing the thumb inside the front teeth is a sign of contempt.

THE HANDSHAKE

"I love a hand that meets my own with a grasp that causes some sensation," wrote Frances Sargent Osgood (Locke), a 19th-century American poet.

Clasping, or grasping a person's hand, is a sign of friendliness. In earlier times it meant the absence of hostility, as it indicated a lack of weapons. Clasping hands can signify allegiance or union with each other. Symbolically, shaking hands forms a cross, or ankh, the ancient Egyptian symbol of life.

The handshake, however, is associated more with Western cultures than with other parts of the globe. To the Western world shaking hands with a person is more than a gesture of greeting. It can leave a lasting impression. First impressions are vitally important, and that first contact often begins with a handshake.

An individual's hands placed together, rather than offered in handshake, implies deferment to a greater power and allegiance. Eastern and Buddhist cultures use this gesture as a means of showing courtesy to other people when greeting them.

Traditionally, the Chinese do not show their hands in a greeting of respect. In China, the right hand stands for yang and strength, and the left hand, yin, is the hand of honor.

Your first introduction to a person's palm usually comes from a handshake, and it can tell you many things. Have you ever shaken hands with a "wet fish" or a "dishrag" and judged them accordingly? If so, you've already dabbled in a little palmistry.

If you shake hands with a person whose palm feels moist, don't sell them short. If the hand is warm as well as moist, you have met someone who cares about other people, often to the point where they worry unnecessarily about pleasing others.

SWEATY PALMS

Sweat ducts and glands are found in great numbers on the hands and can become activated by nervousness. One woman, a beautiful redhead, said she always dreaded being asked to dance because of her sweaty palms. The more she worried about it, the more her palms would sweat. People sitting at a desk in an Internal Revenue Service office awaiting an audit probably have sweaty palms too, but it's only temporary.

Some palmists consider the four astrological elements of water, earth, air and fire when reading the palm. Therefore, a cold, moist palm represents water; a warm, moist hand represents earth; a cold, dry palm is air; and a hot, dry palm is fire. However, since these can be temporary conditions, they cannot be relied on to tell you much about the permanent temperament of a person.

Walter C. Alvarez, M.D., writes in "Live at Peace with Your Nerves" that people are affected differently when they're nervous. Nervous systems affect different parts of the body. Another person may be just as nervous as the one with sweaty palms, but they have no physical reaction.

With the redhead, it happened all the time. Upon examining her hand, other markings indicated an insatiable desire to please everyone. This led to her nervousness and sweaty palms. By changing her way of thinking, she could overcome the sweaty-palm syndrome. In this way, palmistry can be used as a guide to improve a person's self-esteem.

People with sweaty palms are afraid they might hurt someone else's feelings or make a displeasing impression. Yes, they are worry-warts, possibly shy, and often lacking self-confidence, but it is mainly the other person's feelings they are concerned with. Some learn that they can't please everyone, begin to assert themselves and their hands stop sweating.

The cold, sweaty hand is a different story. These people are also insecure, but to the point of being completely wrapped up in their feelings of inadequacy. They don't have the time, regardless of how kind and unassuming they may be, to worry about anyone else.

HARD AND SOFT HANDS

Don't think that just because a person's hand feels soft, they are more vulnerable than someone with a firmer hand. Some of the strongest-willed and most tyrannical people have *soft, spongy* hands. Not all people with soft hands are tyrants, but one of their outstanding traits will be stubbornness.

A palm should feel elastic to the touch and be fairly warm. A little pressure should be felt when grasped, but not to the point that you feel momentarily trapped.

Another extreme is the very *hard, dry* hand. These individuals are probably more vulnerable than might be expected. They are very idealistic and aesthetic; however, the harder and dryer the hand, the more they denigrate opposing viewpoints. They would deny themselves pleasure, even necessities, for what they believe in and expect the same from you.

A *bony, hard* hand, if warm to the touch, can be an ideal hand to have. These are hard-working individuals with a great need to help others. Their major drawback is looking down on someone who isn't as strong as they are.

Smooth-feeling palms, coupled with a warm, genuine handshake and flesh that feels fairly firm, belong to calm, even-tempered individuals. Don't take calluses to mean the person doesn't have a smooth palm. That's just a sign of manual work and should be discounted.

Remember that the way an individual shakes hands, or the way the hand feels, may be temporary. They may have had a bad day, may not be feeling well or may be depressed. Touching a person's palm will give you clues to their mood. Other signs on the palm will give you additional information, such as:

Large hands generally belong to someone who is careful about details. People with small hands tend to think big but don't like fine tuning.

Hands with lots of hair on the back, especially if it runs onto the fingers, have mercurial tempers. Expect a hearty handshake from them because they're usually gregarious. But look out if something makes them mad.

If someone just gives you the tips of their fingers in a handshake, they either have some trouble pressing on their mind or feel threatened by you.

The Color of the Palms

The color of the palms and the lines is determined primarily by the circulation of the blood and is controlled by the mental and physical condition of the individual. Thus, if a person is feeling blue, the hand will be whiter (with a slight bluish tinge). If they're feeling robust, the hand will be pink. If the circulation is too robust, the color will be red. If you rub your palms together briskly, their circulation is increased and they will become redder.

The room temperature, too, plays a role in the color of the hands. Be certain to take all these contributing factors into consideration when noting the color of the hands. Don't assume a palm is always the same—its color can change.

A *slightly pink palm,* warm and fairly elastic to the touch, is the healthiest type of all. These people are in good spirits most of the time and have pleasant personalities.

Pale or almost white palms (usually with a tinge of blue) signify an introverted personality carried to the extreme. These individuals tend to be selfish and unsympathetic. When reading the hand of someone with this colorless indication, check for other markings to see whether this is a significant part of their personality or only temporary, such as a short-term depression.

A *yellowish palm* belongs to an individual with a melancholy nature. Again, look for other signs to see whether it is only temporary.

The reddish palm belongs to the passionate, quick-tempered person. This can be a temporary state. If, however, other markings indicate a quick temperament, the red-colored palm is just another indicator of this.

THE COLOR OF THE LINES

The color of the lines on the hand also tells something of the person's disposition. Lines with a *yellow* tinge indicate a tendency toward depression. Lines that are *white* or *blue* in appearance, especially when the palm is stretched, can be a sign of anemia. They can also mean that the person doesn't have much inner life and lacks vitality.

When the color is *florid red,* the person has a volatile temper, or may be consuming foods that are bad for their health. Extremely red lines can also indicate hypertension.

The lines, when stretched, should be slightly red as a sign of the best health and an energetic disposition.

Sometimes the colors of the palm and lines are much like the mood rings of the 1970s that turned various colors when placed on the finger. These colors depend heavily on the person's temperament at the given moment.

Take into consideration that the darker the skin color (due to race), the darker the lines are going to be. The feel of the palm, whether moist or dry, and the color of the lines and the palm itself, can be a temporary condition. It can, however, give you clues to look for when studying other formations and lines. If the condition of the palm and lines matches the disposition shown by other markings, it becomes significant. It is then no longer a temporary manifestation.

CHAPTER FIVE

The Mounts of the Hand

THE *MOUNTS* OF THE HAND are pads, or raised portions, on the palm that appear beneath the fingers, below the thumb and running down the side of the palm under the little finger (see Fig. 22).

The puffiness, firmness or flatness of these mounts tell a story about the person all by themselves. An absence of these puffy mounts, producing a "flat hand," demonstrates a cold nature and one lacking energy. The mounts should be firm and elastic to the touch.

Certain mounts, however, will be more predominant on individual hands, and this tells a great deal about them.

When the mounts are elevated, they create a hollow in the center of the palm, forming what is called the Quadrangle and the Great Triangle, which will be dealt with at the end of this chapter.

The Mount of Venus, lying beneath the thumb, is the largest mount and generally lends the most intrigue to those having their palms read because it tells about the passionate nature of the person. It is the mount most people have heard about, and the one about which they are the most curious.

Women almost always ask, "Do my hands say I'm passionate?" Perhaps they suspect there's a tiger lying beneath their cool demeanors that despite the alleged sexual revolution has never been turned loose.

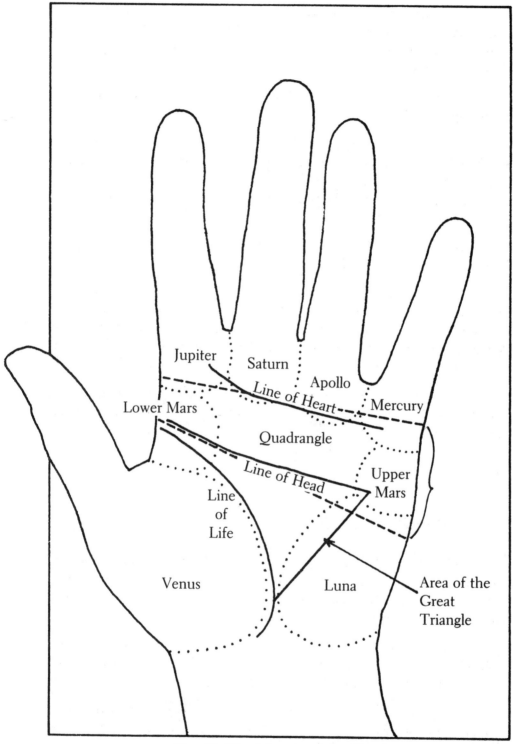

FIG. 22: The Mounts of the Hand

One woman, a forty-two-year-old Tarot reader, showed me her palm and said, "Venus is kinda' flat, huh?" I had known this woman for some time and knew that she had had many lovers and lived an exciting, rather offbeat life.

I laughed and said, "Yes, it's a little flat, but your Mount of Luna makes up for it."

Her Mount of Luna, on the little-finger side of the hand and opposite Venus, was exceptionally firm and puffy—much more pronounced than Venus, which made me tell her, "Since Luna, when it is well formed, gives its owner a vivid imagination, what you lack in passion you make up for with your great ideas."

She acknowledged the truth of my statement with, "I'm never bored and neither are my lovers."

A person who's interested in making a living with their artistic talents may lament that their Mount of Apollo, lying beneath the ring finger and indicating a love of the arts, isn't well-formed. Often a long finger of Apollo makes up for the lacking mount. Other signs on the hand may indicate that the person is a hard worker who never gives up.

The mounts are also linked by name to the planets and gods and goddesses of Graeco-Roman mythology. Some palmists, combining astrology with palmistry, consider that the mounts are under the influence of those planets according to their degree of development. These planetary meanings are similar to their mythological attributes.

THE MOUNT OF VENUS

The *Mount of Venus*, like other mounts on the palm and fingers, is named after a Roman goddess. Venus is associated with her Greek counterpart, Aphrodite, the goddess of love, beauty and marriage. She is also linked to other fertility and love goddesses.

Although most ancient literature and mythology use the name Aphrodite, she is primarily known to Westerners as Venus, perhaps because of the familiarity with the Venus de Milo.

Like Venus, who represented many attributes associated with women, some noble and some not, the mount can stand for either wanton sensuality or concern for mankind.

Aphrodite's birth was given a dual character by the Greeks. In one tradition she was born only of the god Uranus, representing a celestial, spiritual nature. In the other, she was born of a god and goddess and stands for wanton sexuality. Therefore, the Mount of Venus can represent either the spiritual or sensual nature of a person.

This mount, which is surrounded by the Line of Life in a half-circle that begins beneath the index finger and ends near the thumb side of the wrist, should be elastic to the touch and not abnormally large. When exceptionally elevated and flabby, it indicates a sensual nature that is out of control.

The Mount of Venus is usually fuller than the other mounts and when firm and elastic, indicates good health, affection for others, the capacity to love deeply, an attraction to the opposite sex, love of life and an appreciation of beauty. It doesn't promise success with the opposite sex, but certainly leaves the door open to that possibility.

When this mount is narrow, with the Line of Life closer to the thumb but still full and firm, it can be a healthy sign but lacking in passion. Perhaps the person is too cautious.

When the mount is narrow and flat, the person lacks energy, may seem somewhat cold in nature and is seldom attracted to the opposite sex. This doesn't mean they're gay, just that they can do fine without the opposite sex.

THE MOUNT OF LUNA

The Mount of Luna lies opposite Venus, on the little-finger side of the palm. It is named after a Roman goddess of the moon identified with the Greek goddess Selene, who is also identified with the Greek Artemis and the Roman Diana. These goddesses often represented chastity or childbirth (in some mythologies Luna was associated with the death of infant girls) and were personified as huntresses in Greek mythology.

In classical mythology, the moon goddesses were mostly worshipped by women. Some mythologists associate this ancient worship of the moon with women's menstrual cycle.

Luna doesn't lend as much passion to the nature as Venus, but indicates a vivid imagination when well formed. It is outstanding on the hands of romantics, idealists and those with well-developed imaginations. Artists and writers frequently have this mount well developed, as testament to their imaginative and creative abilities.

Men and women who have well-developed Mounts of Luna, whether or not they are involved in the arts, generally love the outdoors and have an appreciation of nature. They tend to be idealistic and sympathetic.

The Mount of Luna is associated with the unconscious, or psychic forces of the personality, and thus puts us in touch with the collective unconscious, which has strong ties to the earth and other people, including our ancestors.

When in control, Luna can benefit a good hand, but as she represents the imagination, she can indicate an individual who walks the fine line between fantasy and reality—hence the term "lunacy."

A well-developed Luna can be an asset unless other markings indicate a melancholy nature (to be covered in subsequent chapters). With negative markings, a well-developed Luna can indicate suicidal tendencies, complete dependence on the opposite sex for feelings of happiness or a tendency to let fantasy outweigh rational thought.

THE MOUNT OF JUPITER

The Mount of Jupiter lies at the base of the first finger. When well developed, it represents a desire for power, control, ambition and the ability to manage others. It is an excellent sign to have.

Jupiter, or Jove, the Roman counterpart of Zeus, ruled over the gods and humanity. He is associated with power and is frequently depicted with thunder and lightning. He once destroyed the world with a violent flood. Jupiter was an important god in the military and public life of the Romans.

High-ranking military officers frequently have this mount well developed, as testament to their desire to lead. It can also be found on the hands of people who are at the forefront of new movements—those not afraid to speak out. I've seen it on the hands of men and women of every persuasion, and if other markings on the hand are good, it is an indicator of leadership ability, whether as head of a business concern or in a small group dedicated to a new cause.

When the first finger is exceptionally long, the person is overly ambitious at the expense of others. They want to be the boss at all costs. This is especially so if the Mount of Saturn, next to it (the middle finger), is not developed at all.

THE MOUNT OF SATURN

The Mount of Saturn lies beneath the middle finger and indicates a love of solitude and music when well developed. Saturn is the equivalent of Cronus, a Roman god associated with agriculture. As Roman mythology gave way to the Greek Kronos, he became a more powerful figure. The Romans built temples of worship to their gods, thus institutionalizing them, whereas the Greeks envisioned them as more powerful, existing everywhere in the heavens and earth.

When the Mount of Saturn is raised and the middle finger is exceptionally long, these people can become melancholy and perhaps depressed. Their anger at the injustices of the world turns inward to the dark corners of their minds, rather than outward to actions that could alleviate the suffering they worry so much about.

THE MOUNT OF APOLLO

The Mount of Apollo lies at the base of the ring finger; when elevated and firm, it indicates an appreciation of beauty. This is often found on the hands of artists and those who have an appreciation of the arts. When other markings on the hand are favorable, it indicates success in the artistic professions.

Apollo, the sun god, associated with music, poetry, prophecy and medicine in classical Greek mythology, is identified with Helios, an earlier Greek sun god. Apollo is also the twin brother of the moon goddess Artemis, who is referred to as Luna in some mythologies.

Hands with a well-developed Mount of Apollo frequently have the Mount of Luna well elevated also. This is a good sign. It blends the love of art as shown by Apollo with the imagination of Luna.

THE MOUNT OF MERCURY

The Mount of Mercury, beneath the little finger, is the Roman name for the Greek god Hermes. Mercury was worshipped in Rome as a god of trading and profit and was considered a bringer of luck. In Arab manuscripts, Mercury is depicted as a scribe.

The Mount of Mercury, when well developed, indicates a desire for change. People with this sign usually have a good sense of humor, are generous with laughter and love to be around people. But they have quick tempers. If other markings are favorable, they have the ability to make money.

If the other markings are unfavorable, they will ceaselessly chase excitement, change and money. If the mount itself is in excess, it signifies a greedy nature.

THE MOUNT OF UPPER MARS

The Mount of Upper Mars, which lies below the Mount of Mercury, is often unnoticed by itself. Rather, it is a continuation of Mercury and Luna that simply makes the side of the hand appear elevated from its beginning on Mercury down through Luna.

The Greek counterpart of Mars is Ares. He was originally an agricultural deity and stood for regeneration and growth. As the Roman people turned from farming to war, Mars became associated with the trappings of battle—combativeness, contentiousness, chauvinism and sturdiness.

A well-developed Upper Mars lends itself to energy and enthusiasm for life. When excessively large, it indicates a combative nature.

THE MOUNT OF LOWER MARS

The Mount of Lower Mars lies at the topmost area within the Line of Life, next to the Mount of Venus. When puffy (it will appear creased), it indicates a fighting spirit. It is found on the hands of people actively involved in sports, especially those that call for a certain amount of physical pain. When unusually large, it indicates a quarrelsome nature.

Men with a well-developed Mount of Lower Mars can usually tolerate a great deal of physical pain. It is rare on a woman's hand and indicates a very hardy constitution. They usually have fewer complications in childbirth, or at least hide their pain more readily.

Why this mount is rare on a woman's hand is a mystery to me. It has been shown that women can tolerate pain as much as men and may even have a greater capacity to endure it. But men have been conditioned not to show pain, whereas women have been allowed to. Perhaps Lower Mars is simply the ability to hide pain; this is an area that will need further study by students of palmistry.

Scientists have demonstrated, however, that individuals have different pain thresholds, which are in part determined by the development of their nervous systems during gestation.

WELL-DEVELOPED MOUNTS

Although it is sometimes difficult to judge markings such as mounts from palm prints, the accompanying print picked up the exceedingly well-developed mounts on the hand of Vicki B., a forty-five-year-old businesswoman (Fig. 23).

Outstanding is the full Mount of Lower Mars lying inside the Line of Life, which indicates the physical strength of this woman, who has made her fortune fixing up houses for sale and rent.

Vicki and her husband (now deceased) worked side by side on the homes. She's adept at throwing heavy roofing material on her shoulder, carrying it up a ladder and patching a roof. Vicki is a small woman, so her large hands are quite notable.

Her Mounts of Luna and Venus are also well developed, making her an energetic, enthusiastic person, capable of sharing an abundance of love and passion.

After reading the chapters on major and minor lines, you may want to check out her Lines of Apollo, Fate and Heart. It is a well-marked, square hand, belonging to a strong woman, but one whose heart will always rule her head.

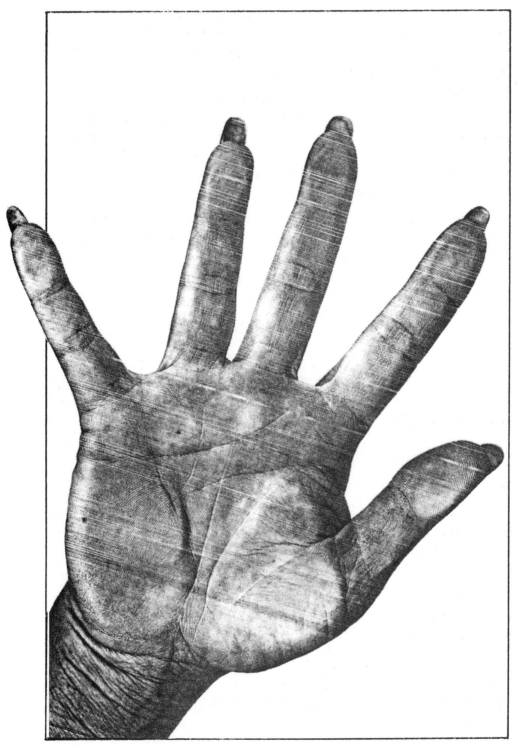

Fig. 23: Well-Developed Mounts (Vicki B.)

THE QUADRANGLE

The Quadrangle, that flat area in the center of the upper portion of the palm, lying between the Lines of Heart and Head, should be smooth, with few lines crossing it. When fairly even and not too narrow in the middle, it shows an even disposition and intelligence—a person who is trusting, accepting, nonjudgmental and broad-minded. It is an indicator of how you view the world internally.

As the center narrows, so does your view of the world. The narrower it becomes, the more bigoted, judgmental and stingy is the person.

When the Quadrangle is excessively broad, these people become too broad-minded for their own good.

A WELL-BALANCED QUADRANGLE

The following print (Fig. 24) is that of Tim A., college professor and peace activist, who lives in a mountain community and sometimes bicycles twenty miles to work.

It is a clear example of a well-balanced Quadrangle, showing an even disposition and intelligence. Although he is concerned about nuclear armament, he isn't cynical and remains optimistic that the work he does will have an effect on mankind.

It is unusual to find these particular markings on a predominantly square hand with square fingers, which indicates a conservative nature. He is, however, an independent thinker, as shown by the little finger separated from the ring finger.

After studying the major lines on the hand (Chapter Six), you may want to return to this print and study the formation of the Lines of Life and Head.

THE GREAT TRIANGLE

The Great Triangle lies between the Line of Life and the Line of Head, with the narrow end beneath Jupiter and the wide end opening on the Mount of Luna. It should cover a good portion of the central, flat part

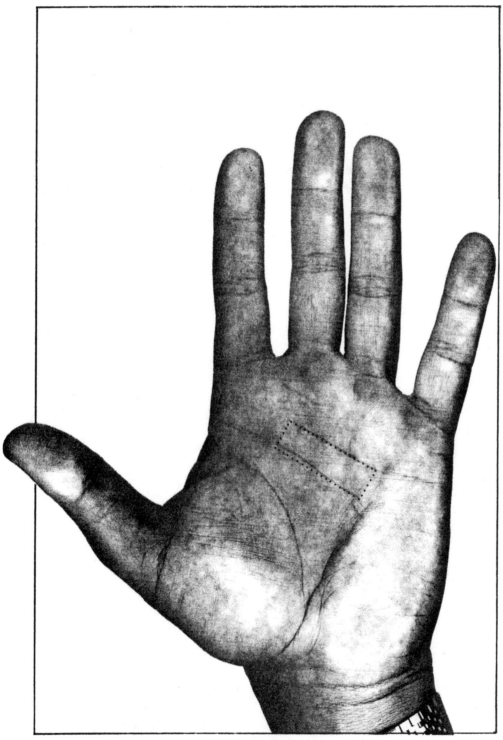

FIG. 24: A Well-Balanced Quadrangle (Tim A.)

of the palm. When it does, it denotes intelligence and good health, especially if the lines forming it are clear and deep.

When it is narrow, and the surrounding lines are weak, broken or chained, it tells of a weaker nature and not one given to good fortune.

FINGERTIP PADS

Pads on the inside of the fingertips indicate tactful people who truly care about the feelings of others and will go out of their way to avoid hurting anyone.

CHAPTER SIX

Major Lines of the Hand

T<small>HE</small> <small>MAJOR LINES</small> of the hand include the *Line of Life, Line of Head, Line of Heart* and *Line of Fate*. There are a variety of beginnings and endings to these lines (as shown in the broken lines on the accompanying charts), and each variation tells something different about the person.

The Line of Life, which encircles the Mount of Venus, doesn't tell how long a person will live, but is rather an indicator of the quality of life in store for the person. A Line of Life that appears to stop part way down the palm, if it's deep and clear, indicates a reckless nature. If it's short and weak, they're not interested in the world around them. A long Line of Life that is deep and clear indicates vitality and a robust outlook on life.

A person's Line of Life can branch out to other parts of the palm (chiefly the Mount of Luna), where it indicates a love of travel. Or it can curve even farther into the Mount of Luna, indicating an exploratory nature.

Many times, in dealing with a short Line of Life, I'm reminded of a couple I once interviewed during the time I worked as a reporter. They had been married for seventy-five years. I was certain they would have interesting things to say about their life together and their long individual lives.

I couldn't have been more wrong.

I used all of my interviewing skills but learned from them only that they had never traveled, didn't belong to any church, didn't read much and never had, watched a little TV, didn't have many friends and never had, subscribed to no special diet and had no favorite foods, no hobbies, a daughter who visited once in a while, and didn't even own a dog or cat. They had no explanation for why their marriage had lasted so long, didn't care about world events, kept the house fairly clean and didn't do any particular form of exercise.

As I was heading for the door, anxious to leave, the wife said to me, "I don't know why we've lived so long or been married as long as we have. We've never done anything."

By the time I got back to the office, I was thoroughly depressed. I wish now that I had asked to see their palms. I suspect they had weak, short Lines of Life despite their ninety-odd years of living on this planet.

Naturally, it is best when lines are deep, smooth and unbroken, but this is not always the case. Some people worry because their lines appear fainter than those of their friends. Generally, the lines are lighter on conic, psychic and philosophic hands. They appear bolder on square and spatulate hands and convey the same meaning when this is taken into consideration.

The *length* of the lines will vary from hand to hand, depending on the shape of the hand. It is natural to find a long Line of Head on the conic, philosophic and psychic hand, and for it to be shorter on the square and spatulate. When it appears to be exceptionally long on the square or spatulate, it takes on more meaning.

For example, an unusually long Line of Head on a square hand would indicate greater intelligence than it would on a philosophic hand.

The upper portions of the hand represent the *spiritual* side of the person and the lower, the *material*. Thus, if the Lines of Heart and Head are low on the palm, the person is more materialistic than if they appear higher up.

By itself, a line only shows intellectual and emotional tendencies which must be backed up elsewhere for a complete understanding of the person.

Forked lines have greater power than single lines, and minor lines rising from a major line add power to the line from which they spring. *Descending* lines crimp the strength of the major lines.

Bearing these facts in mind, we'll proceed to the first major line.

THE LINE OF LIFE

The Line of Life is found encircling the Mount of Venus and generally comes close to touching the middle of the palm as it curves down the hand toward the thumb side.

The Line of Life is more indicative of the physical life of a person. A long Line of Life, albeit a thin one, can be found on the dullest people.

This line should be as free from breaks as possible, for these would indicate interruptions in the normal flow of life. Its usual starting point is beneath or on the Mount of Jupiter (1) (see Fig. 25) and it ends near the wrist on the thumb side of the palm (A). However, there are numerous variations.

When the line originates high on Jupiter (2), it indicates energy from early childhood.

A Line of Life ending in a *fork* (B) indicates a restless nature and a desire for change. If other markings on the hand are good, this individual likes challenges.

If the Line of Life ends toward Luna, on the other side of the palm (C), the person loves to travel and may eventually live in a foreign country.

When the Line of Life becomes lighter near its end, or less frequently, farther up in the palm, the person's energy or life force is fading. In the case of a waning Line of Life, look for *backup lines* (D) running along and inside the line. These add strength to the fading line.

The shorter and weaker the line, the more frail and timid the person.

When the line is *chained*—that is, broken and made up of small links—it indicates illness at the time* the breaks occur. The severity of this illness is lessened if there are other lines running parallel to the break inside the Line of Life on the Mount of Venus.

A Line of Life connected to the Line of Head, which is the second most prominent line running beneath the fingers across the palm, indicates an intelligent but cautious nature. Everything must be weighed and measured before these people will proceed with an endeavor. They dwell

*How time is determined in the palm is explained in the Appendix.

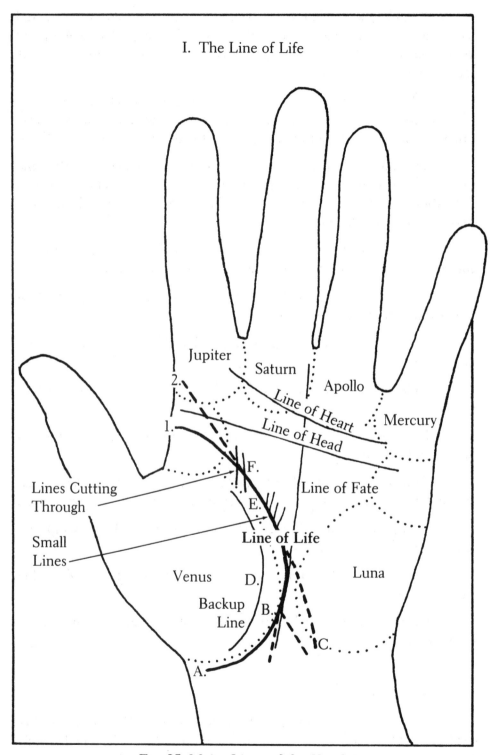

FIG. 25: Major Lines of the Hand

on the obstacles, rather than the possibilities. This could also be connected to the belief of some palm-readers that when the Lines of Life and Head are joined at the beginning, it creates an intense attachment to the parents that lasts into adulthood.

When all three lines—Life, Head and Heart (which lies above the Line of Head)—are *joined together* at the start, it indicates a surly nature. Such people are suspicious of change, and distrust the judgment of others.

The opposite is true of a Line of Life that is *separated* from the Line of Head. This person is optimistic and eager to try new ventures. If this separation is excessively wide, however, the person is a daredevil and often fails to look before leaping.

Small lines rising from, but not inside, the Line of Life (E) indicate success. The direction they take tells the nature of this success.

Heading toward Jupiter, the index finger, they mean a promotion at work or continued education.

Aimed at Apollo, the ring finger (see Fig. 25), they promise success in the arts.

Going toward Mercury, the little finger, they intimate a monetary reward.

Lines that cut through the Line of Life are unfortunate signs and usually indicate interferences.

Cutting through and heading into the Line of Fate, which runs up the center of the palm, they signify interference by business acquaintances.

Cutting through and touching the Line of Head (F), they indicate that someone will block ideas.

Cutting through or touching the Line of Heart, they spell trouble with the love life.

Heading toward Apollo, they show that a scandal of some sort is brewing.

THE LINE OF HEAD

The Line of Head is located beneath the fingers, between the Line of Heart and the Line of Life. This line represents the intellect and reveals both the direction it will take and the individual's potential.

The Line of Head frequently varies from the left hand to the right and can give many clues to the person's inherited characteristics and the environment in which they were raised.

I've been told by some people, when I've asked to see both of their hands, that they had previously had their hands read by a Gypsy fortune-teller who used only the left hand.

I can only guess that the Gypsies, with their long tradition of palm-reading, still go on the supposition that the child's hand, whether right or left, will be similar to the parents', and that the child is destined to follow in the parents' footsteps. This is no longer the case in our modern society. Another reason could be that the left hand is closer to the heart.

On a right-handed person, the left hand signifies the talents, tendencies and potentials they were born with; on a left-handed person, this is shown in the right hand.

If someone tells you they're ambidextrous, the main reading is done on the right hand.

I usually take a quick glance at the left hand (of a right-handed person) to see if there are any major line variations between hands.

The Line of Head will often be stronger in the right hand, indicating that the person is making the best use of their inherent talents. Occasionally I run across the opposite of this. I tell a person they're not living up to their potential and try to find the reason why.

When the Line of Head *forks at its ending*, it tells which parent had the stronger influence on the person. If the lower fork on a woman's hand is longer, she takes after her father. If the upper fork is longest, she's more like her mother. The opposite is true for a man.

When the lines of the fork are of *equal length*, this is a person who can see both sides of an issue. It's as if there is a balance between the father and mother, or the male-female side of themselves.

Many people are irritated to find they have a number of their parents' characteristics. This may be because the father is tied to convention or the mother came from a generation of housewives and the adult child wants no part of that type of life. However, the parents may once have dreamed of lives far different from the way theirs developed and may be happy to see the change in their child—although they may be bewildered by it.

I have found that many people limit themselves, but the hands tell what's hidden in their hearts. I seldom divulge anything they don't already suspect themselves, but the Line of Head is a dead giveaway.

BEGINNINGS

The Line of Head generally starts in the center of the Mount of Jupiter, near the beginning of the Line of Life, or from the Mount of Upper Mars within the Line of Life (see Fig. 26).

It most often ends about three-quarters of the way across the palm, heading toward the little-finger side of the hand. At this length, it portends intelligence and a logical mind.

If it runs less than halfway across the palm, it indicates a single train in the thought process. This is the person who knows a lot about a little. If they're a cook, that's all they can talk about.

Where the Line of Head begins and ends is of utmost importance. When it begins near Jupiter, the person is ambitious, able to manage other people, energetic and seems to know where they are headed. This is even more pronounced if it slightly touches the Line of Life at its beginning (1). When it is separated from the Line of Life (2), the person has the same characteristics, but tends to take more risks.

When the Line of Head is closely connected to the Line of Life at its beginning (3), it shows a tendency to be overly cautious. These people usually don't rise to their full potential and often become bitter about it. But if they become aware of their overcautious nature and listen to fellow workers and friends when they're working out problems, they can make the best of their ambitions.

The Line of Head beginning within the Line of Life (4) in the area of the Mount of Lower Mars is the least favorable of all the signs. This person is irritable with others and always ready for an argument. Fortunately, I run across very few people with this formation.

Equally important is where the Line of Head ends.

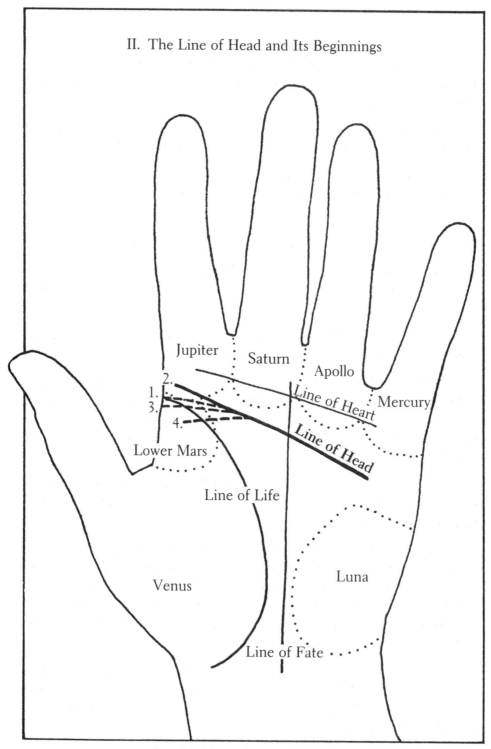

II. The Line of Head and Its Beginnings

Jupiter Saturn Apollo

Line of Heart Mercury

2.
1.
3.
4.

Line of Head

Lower Mars

Line of Life

Venus Luna

Line of Fate

Fig. 26: Major Lines of the Hand

ENDINGS

When the line is *long* and runs *straight* across the hand (A) (see Fig. 27), the person is single-minded and will work on a problem until it's done. They usually have an aptitude for science and mathematics. If I were selecting a tax accountant, I'd want his Line of Head to be fairly straight.

If it runs straight across the hand, but isn't quite so long, the person's stubbornness will interfere with the projects they undertake.

When the Line of Head *forks* at its ending (B), the person is well balanced and good at seeing both sides of an issue.

If the lower fork ends on the Mount of Luna (C), the person has a vivid imagination, but one tempered by the practical side of their nature.

When the Line of Head ends farther down on Luna (D), the imagination runs wild at times, but is usually put to good use, such as in writing or painting.

A Line of Head first *curving down* and then heading for Upper Mars (E) signifies success in financial matters.

When the Line of Head curves dramatically downward (F), the person has a tendency toward depression and possibly suicide, depending on other markings in the palm. Frequently this suicidal tendency can be found on the hands of other family members. This lends credibility to the theory that some people inherit a tendency toward suicide.

The key word here is "some" people. Suicide can be the result of a dysfunctional family, or seemingly unsolvable problems at any age, and is not always an inherited characteristic.

"It's a constant combination of what one can cope with plus the environmental stresses," according to Michael T. Peck, a Los Angeles psychotherapist who specializes in youth suicide. He also works with the Institute for Studies of Destructive Behaviors and the Suicide Prevention Center in Los Angeles. Peck adds that the basis for being suicidal is "being hopeless and helpless."

There are unlimited contributing factors to these feelings of hopelessness and helplessness. Not only do environmental factors play a role, but studies indicate that part of the rise in teen suicide may be due to undiagnosed schizophrenia.

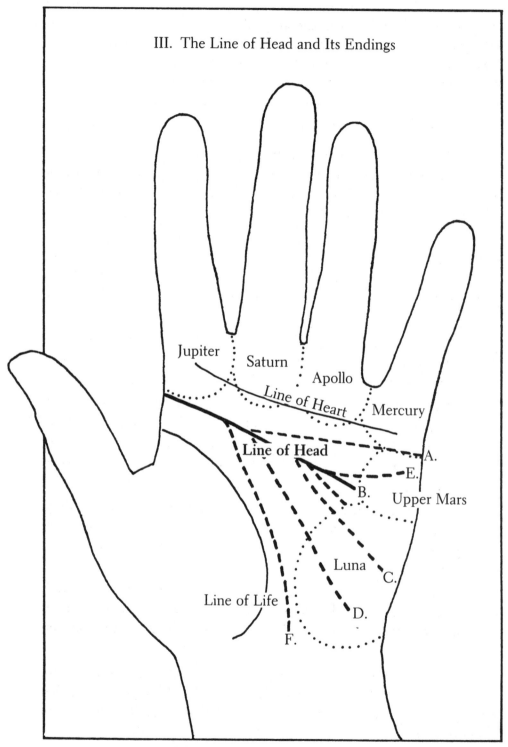

FIG. 27: Major Lines of the Hand

Therefore, when you encounter this particular sloping Line of Head, it should be dealt with seriously. The left hand of the person being read (if they're right-handed) should be checked to see whether the Line of Head appears the same on both hands. If so, the propensity for depression or suicide may be an inherited characteristic.

THE GENETIC FACTOR

Genetic research begun in the late 1950s and early '60s has contradicted long-held beliefs that a child's personality is completely shaped by its environment; indications are that heredity accounts for up to fifty percent of a child's temperament.

David W. Fulker, a researcher at the Institute of Behavior Genetics, University of Colorado, says that parents who are genetically disposed to such traits as altruism or aggression not only pass on the genes favorable to those traits but are also more likely to provide environments that enhance them.

Fulker says that aggressive personalities were found in three successive generations during research conducted at the University of London Institute of Psychiatry, in which he took part.

This research, which is taking place all over the world and which includes other personality traits, does not exclude environment as a contributing factor, however. The new challenge for parents is to learn to nurture their child's individual temperament, according to researchers and child psychologists.

Genetic influence on temperament is not quite the same as say, genetic influence on height. Rather, the genes code for production of certain structures in the brain and nervous system, which in turn affect the nervous system and hence, behavior.

Therefore, when I see an extremely sloping Line of Head, I inform the person. Usually I'll begin by asking them whether any close members of their family suffer from chronic depression, or whether any have attempted suicide.

As I stated in the Introduction, palmists who tell people they're going to die young or have a car accident don't rate very high with me. But when you see the potential for suicide and don't talk about it openly, you might be avoiding something that could save a person's life.

More often than not, when I've been open about the subject, the person has acknowledged that a close family member did indeed attempt suicide. That leaves the door open to tell them about their own potential and to suggest that they see a therapist when the need arises. It is not the task of palm-readers to try to heal anyone. That should be left to professionals.

ADDITIONAL LINE OF HEAD INFLUENCES

A short Line of Head that ends halfway out into the palm makes its owner extremely materialistic.

When the Line of Head is deeper and more pronounced than the Line of Heart, the head rules the heart.

If the line is chained or wavy, the person is a procrastinator and has difficulty making decisions.

When the Lines of Head and Heart are combined into one line, generally running straight across the hand, the person will tend to be fanatical and very jealous. When the lines are joined, it usually has a broad, deep appearance.

The Line of Head is usually longer on conic, philosophic and psychic hands than it is on square or spatulate ones.

Breaks in the Line of Head indicate a fatalistic view of life, usually brought about by a tragic occurrence in the person's life from which they never quite recover.

AN INTERESTING LINE OF HEAD

The following hand (Fig. 28) belongs to thirty-year-old Danile B. and illustrates the Line of Head separated from the Line of Life. This is the hand of a daredevil, since the space is quite wide between the two lines.

It is a spatulate hand, the hand of an inventor with an independent nature. Fortunately, the lines on this hand are good—the Head and Heart are well balanced and the Line of Life is deep. It is a strong hand with a good thumb, but it is the hand of someone who will have difficulty settling down to one career. Because of her spatulate hand, Danile is full of ideas.

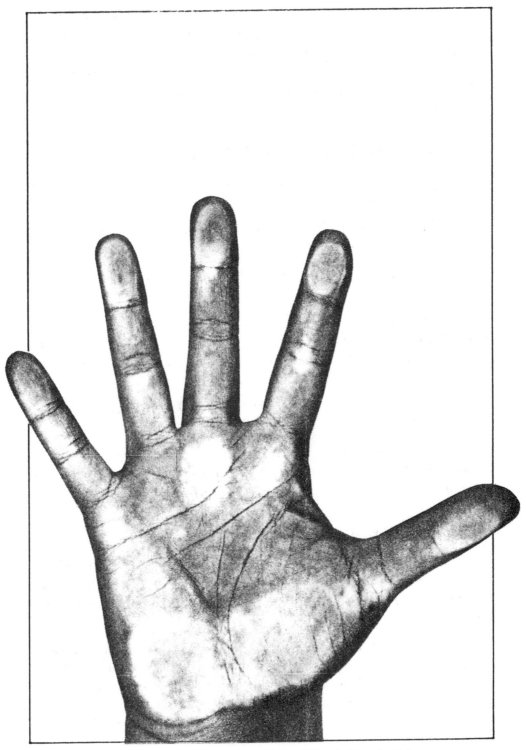

Fig. 28: An Interesting Line of Head (Danile B.)

Due to the Line of Head that is separated from the Line of Life, however, she takes many risks.

She will not have a steady career until her mid-thirties. Note the Line of Fate beginning in the middle of the palm and running parallel to and outside the Line of Life. Danile will more than likely be in business for herself or with a partner and will prove to be very adept at handling the financial end of the enterprise (as shown by the straight Line of Head that nearly makes its way toward Mercury).

THE LINE OF HEART

The Line of Heart offers clues to the way a person accepts or rejects love, how they behave toward the people they love and why.

Psychologists say that poor relationships are at the root of many of the problems facing their clients. This not only involves relationships with the opposite sex, but with parents, family and friends.

The Line of Heart reveals the emotional background of the individual. It is one of the formations that can change dramatically over the course of a person's life. It may begin as a weak line and become strong, indicating early years spent in uncertainty regarding love, or there may be a break in the line showing a traumatic love affair in the person's life. Usually, the Line of Heart will portray the type of love the person is capable of giving in adult life. This in turn is the type of love they will receive.

It is the deep line at the top portion of the palm which ends somewhere beneath the Mount of Mercury (see Fig. 29). Situated *high* on the palm, it shows a pleasant nature. Running closer to the Line of Head, it tells of potentially unhappy relationships, especially in the early part of life.

When quite low on the palm, nearly touching the Line of Head, the heart will always interfere with the person's intellectual and professional life, especially if it is deeper than the Line of Head.

This line, at its best, should be clear and deep but can have branches running from it. It doesn't tell of marriage and affairs, only how the person will relate emotionally to love or the lack of it.

Some palmists refer to the "beginnings" as I have them placed. Others refer to them as the endings or terminations. But the meanings of

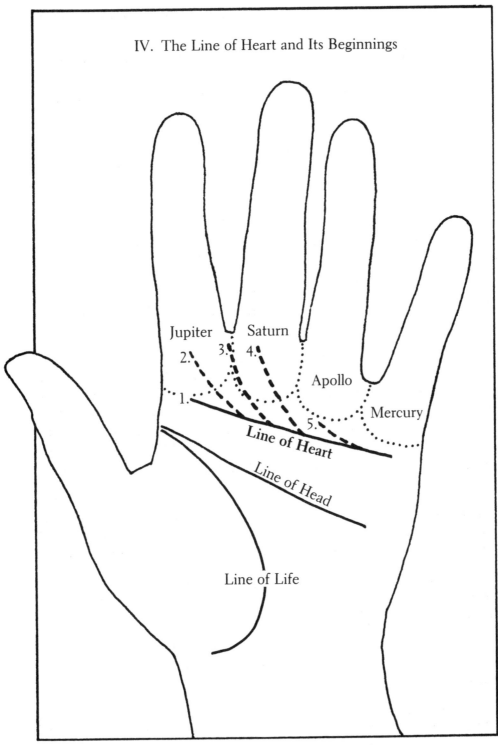

FIG. 29: Major Lines of the Hand

either school are the same. I have come across no explanations for this inconsistency.

The Heart Line doesn't indicate ages at which specific events will take place, as do the Lines of Head, Fate and Life,* so whether a certain portion of the line is referred to as the beginning or ending is of no consequence.

Beginnings

If the Line of Heart begins in the lower portion of the Mount of Jupiter below the index finger (1) (see Fig. 29), the person is true and loyal in their feelings for the opposite sex. Fidelity in marriage will have great meaning to them, but they'll never be a doormat. They'll always retain a certain amount of independence but will consider their relationships a top priority.

The Line of Heart running into the Mount of Jupiter (2), or even farther, into the Jupiter finger, suggests great idealism in marriage or relationships. Remember that Jupiter is the finger of power and authority. These people may give too much of themselves and expect the same in return, only to be disappointed. They are looking for the perfect mate.

When the Line of Heart commences between the Mounts of Jupiter and Saturn (3), these people are more inclined to accept reality and make fewer demands in a relationship. The finger of Saturn and its mount indicate the solitary side of the individual. Even though the line is between the fingers of Saturn and Jupiter, these people look inward when dealing with a mate, rather than seeking their desires in the other person. They can be passionate, caring and are able to develop sustaining relationships.

If the Line of Heart begins under Saturn (4), these individuals may be passionate and loving but a little on the selfish side. They are too much into themselves. It is difficult for these people to "let go and let love." They are not demonstrative, but, given mates who understand them, can be wonderful lovers in private.

When the line is *short*, barely beginning under the ring finger of Apollo (5), and exceedingly broad or chained, the person has little interest in the opposite sex and may even dislike them.

When the line is long, running boldly across a person's palm from

*See Appendix.

side to side, there is a tendency to be jealous and a need to control their mate. This is especially true if the Lines of Heart and Head are combined into one line. When this occurs, the person is inclined to become a religious fanatic. It is as if they can't separate the heart and the mind, which leads to inner turmoil.

Two Heart Lines

The following print (Fig. 30), belonging to Jackie P., is an example of a Heart Line beginning under Jupiter.

The one appearing after it (Fig. 31) is that of an entrepreneur, a man in his late twenties. It is an example of an extremely short Line of Heart.

Other Persuasions of the Heart

Chained Lines of Heart (lines made up of little islands) indicate disappointment in love and tell of a cautious nature. These people don't trust love, even though they seek it desperately. It is as if a portion of their minds remains chained, unable to love freely. Often, only part of the line is chained, indicating that the person has overcome their fear of love.

When crowded by little hairlines rising from the Line of Heart, the person is a flirt. The lines are usually light and airy, like the person's heart. These people glow like light bulbs around the opposite sex, drawing energy from the mounts toward which the hairlines point.

Many lines drooping from the Line of Heart mean trouble with the opposite sex. These lines are aimed at the lower part of the palm, the unconscious, unknown, less certain portion of the hand.

A pale, broad line illustrates a noncaring attitude toward the opposite sex. It is like a crafted line, rather than one of fine art.

Breaks in the Line of Heart show disappointment in the love life, usually brought about by the person's own attitude.

Forks at the beginning of the Line of Heart, that is, with one branch resting on Jupiter and the other on Saturn, indicate an independent nature, one that could have difficulty establishing a lasting relationship. These people live in two worlds—one of independence, the other wanting to form secure bonds—but are torn between the two.

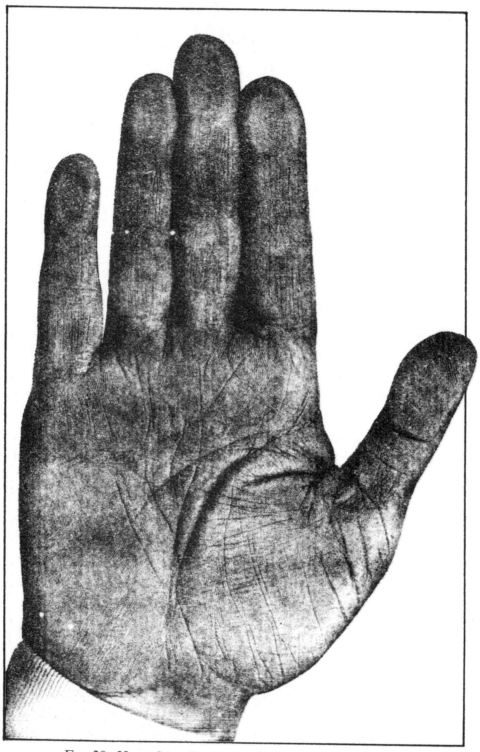

FIG. 30: Heart Line Beginning Under Jupiter (Jackie P.)

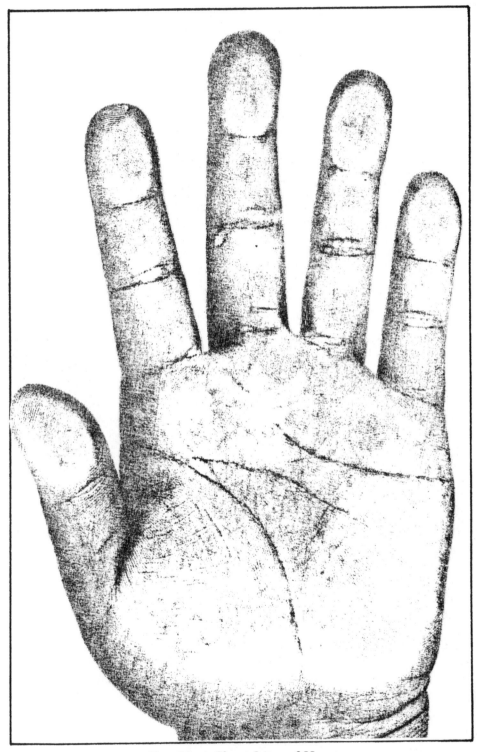

FIG. 31: A Short Line of Heart

A line that is thin and lacking in branches, either heading toward the mounts or drooping downward, means the person is fragile and slightly cold in affections. The line just lies there in all its delicate beauty, doing nothing.

When the Line of Heart is absent altogether, the person may be very sensual but incapable of feeling deep love.

A HEARTY HEART LINE

The following palm-print of Omara C., thirty, is a good example of a strong Line of Heart that begins between the fingers of Jupiter and Saturn (see Fig. 32).

Although it is deep and strong, with no breaks, she has to be careful because this indicates that her heart rules her head. That's because it's stronger than any of the other lines, particularly the Head Line.

In her favor is a lengthy, break-free Line of Head and a good Line of Fate, showing that she will carve out a career for herself despite early setbacks due to the persuasion of the heart.

Success in her career will come in mid-life, after a difficult struggle (see following section on the Fate Line). She has several branches to her Line of Fate, which you can note after reading the following section.

A BROKEN LINE OF HEART

The following print (Fig. 33) illustrates a broken Line of Heart (as well as a broken Line of Head) and bespeaks a life that will be haunted by an unfortunate romance. This young man, a college student, is a steady type of person, not prone to depression, but one who, nevertheless, will let his broken heart color his entire life.

THE LINE OF FATE

The Line of Fate is sometimes called the Line of Saturn, since its most natural place is heading up from the wrist in the direction of Saturn (middle finger). It usually runs parallel to the Line of Life in the lower portion of the hand (see Fig. 34).

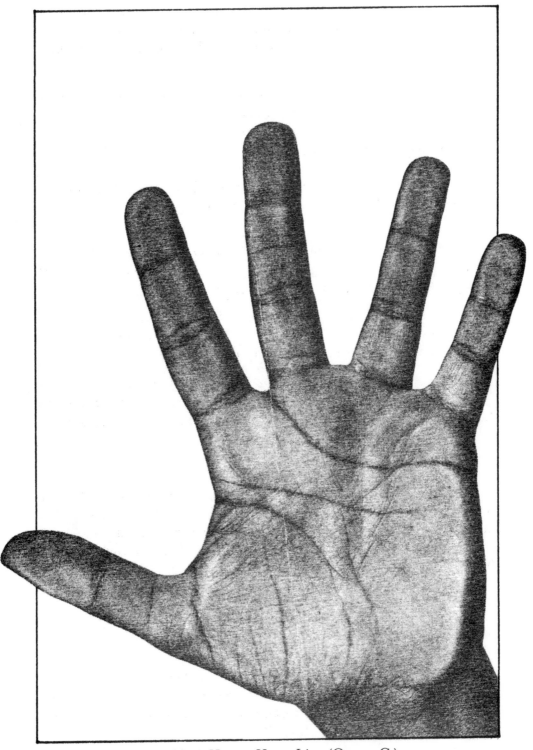

Fig. 32: A Hearty Heart Line (Omara C.)

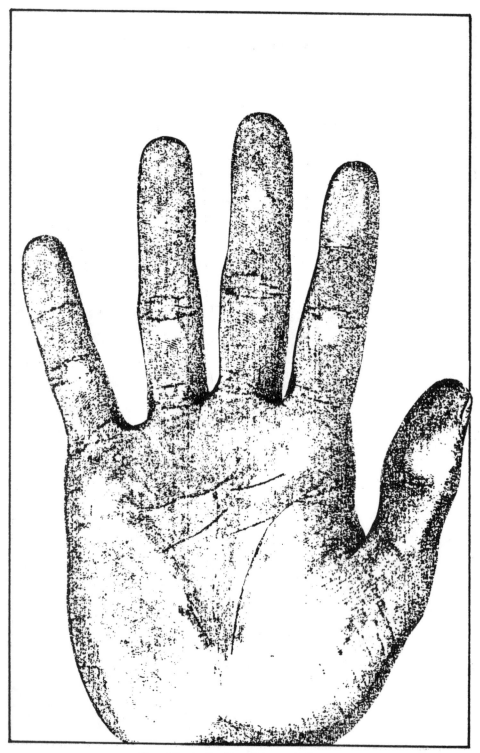

Fig. 33: A Broken Line of Heart

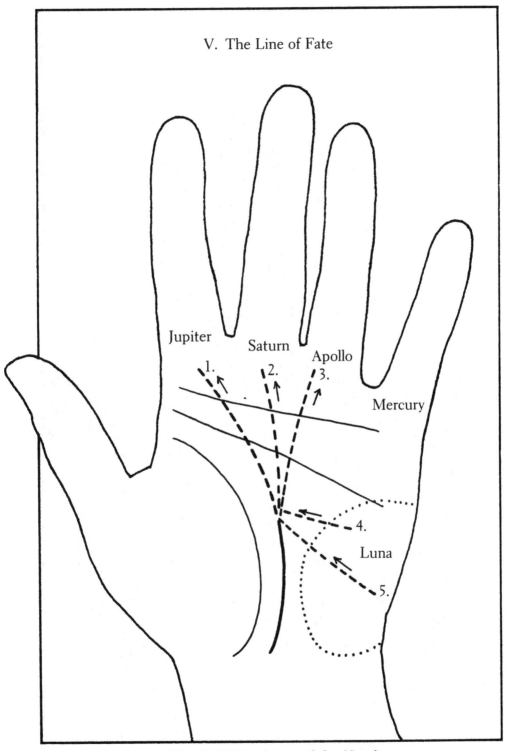

FIG. 34: Major Lines of the Hand

Sometimes it ends high up on the hand near the fingers. Frequently it doesn't travel that far, but ends in the middle of the palm. Actually, when the line appears to stop here, it indicates a late beginning to a career, so it must be seen as heading downward toward the wrist.

There are two major beginnings for the Line of Fate: one at the wrist, heading toward Saturn, and the other, beginning in the middle of the palm and heading down toward the wrist. This can be confusing, but the line is one of the most interesting ones regarding the paths we take in life. Other variations on this will be explained in this section.

The Fate Line speaks more of the person's mental attributes than the physical, which is the domain of the Line of Life. A person can have other lines that appear weak, but a strong Line of Fate will overshadow those weaknesses.

This line indicates the inner persona and how it relates to the outside world. In no other line is it more evident that it's not what happens to us that matters, but how we cope with it. Other lines tell us what some of these occurrences will be. The Fate Line tells us how we will cope with them. While the Fate Line may not run straight up the palm without sending offshoots to other mounts, the vitality of the line is that it picks up the human events surrounding us.

Some people lack a Line of Fate altogether. That doesn't mean they lack a destiny. Some simply don't have the drive to achieve goals and are in limbo waiting for things to happen to them instead of getting out and making them happen.

Frequently, those who lack a Line of Fate depend too much on others. I once read the hand of a woman who had been the mistress of a married man for about thirty years. She had traveled all over (but had no travel lines), had children (which weren't indicated on the hand), had had serious illnesses (which weren't recorded), and yet had lived a rather pleasured life. She also had no Line of Fate. She was quite pleasant to talk to and seemed intelligent.

This hand still remains a puzzle to me. It was as if she were here on this planet, but not *really* here. She lived in a shell, and the events around her played little part in her life.

People who have Lines of Fate cut across with lines of interference, even if they are faint, or with offshoots into unexpected areas, seem more grounded in life and more sociable.

It should be remembered that the Line of Fate will appear stronger on philosophic and conic hands than on square or spatulate ones. The latter two belong to those who aren't great believers in destiny.

This line, or the lack of it, is quite changeable. New shoots can spring up in the course of a person's life, and Lines of Fate can appear where once there were none.

People who have floundered along, dependent on others, probably have no Lines of Fate. On the other hand, I have seen many people who lacked this line in the first part of their lives obtain strong ones in the latter part.

A strong Line of Fate, regardless of where it begins or ends, is an indication of structure in life. People without this line may have great ideas, but they lack the drive and energy to carry them through.

If this line is absent in your palm, it's a good idea to sit down and think about your life—where you want to go and who you want to be.

It is not for me to say which is the "best" direction for a Line of Fate to take. Much depends on the individual's personality, where they're coming from. I like variety, and the individual beginnings and endings, the offshoots and zigzags, add sparkle to a person's life.

When the Line of Fate ends on the Mount of Jupiter (1) (see Fig. 34), it indicates an early talent in the management of people, based on a desire to be the star. Politicians and entertainers frequently have this marking.

If it runs into the finger itself, the person's life will be dominated by the desire for power.

An ending on Saturn (2) shows success in whatever field of endeavor is selected, if the line is strong. If it ends farther up in the finger itself, the person will be overcome by their success to the point of eliminating other aspects of their life.

If the line ends on Apollo (3), it shows interest in the arts. If the line is strong and the mount elevated, success is assured.

When the line starts on the Mount of Luna (4), these people are adept at helping others. They trust their intuition and know when someone is in pain. Caution is needed with this marking, however, because they may give too much of themselves in their desire to help others.

When the Line of Fate begins deep within Luna (5), the person is imbued with a spiritual nature. If the line is strong, they will be able to incorporate this spirituality into their career or life's work. Again, they must be cautious about becoming too involved with the problems of others.

Frequently, the Line of Fate will appear to head in one direction and then send an offshoot in another. These mark career changes.

Your hand will not tell you what kind of vocation you'll undertake, but based on several markings it can tell you what types of work suit you best. The Line of Fate will tell where these talents and inclinations are likely to take you.

OTHER TRICKS OF FATE

Small lines that shoot toward other mounts from the Line of Fate take on the qualities of those mounts (see Fig. 35). Thus, if an offshoot heads toward Apollo (1), that person might find success as an artist.

Branches heading toward Mercury (2) predict financial good fortune.

If the Line of Fate runs beyond the Mount of Saturn into the finger (3), this person will be a zealot about their ambitions and all may not end well. Mothers who dominate their children excessively frequently have this marking.

The Line of Fate is usually stronger on conic, philosophical and psychic hands.

Breaks in the line tell of temporary setbacks in the career but often lead to stronger lines, indicating greater success than the previous position offered.

A double Line of Fate indicates a dual career.

When the Line of Fate appears to rise late in life from the Mount of Upper Mars (4), success will come late after a troubled life.

When it rises from the Line of Heart (5), success will come only after a struggle.

Breaks in the line with nothing to take their place mean an uncertain career.

When the Line of Fate travels down the hand, closely connected to

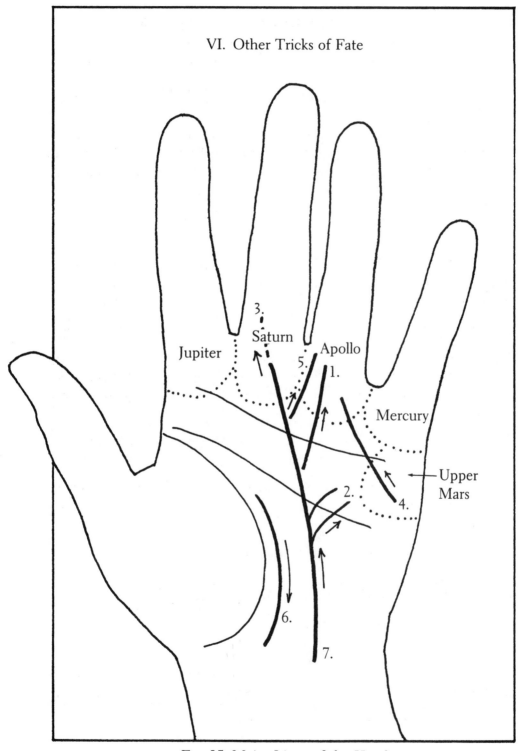

FIG. 35: Major Lines of the Hand

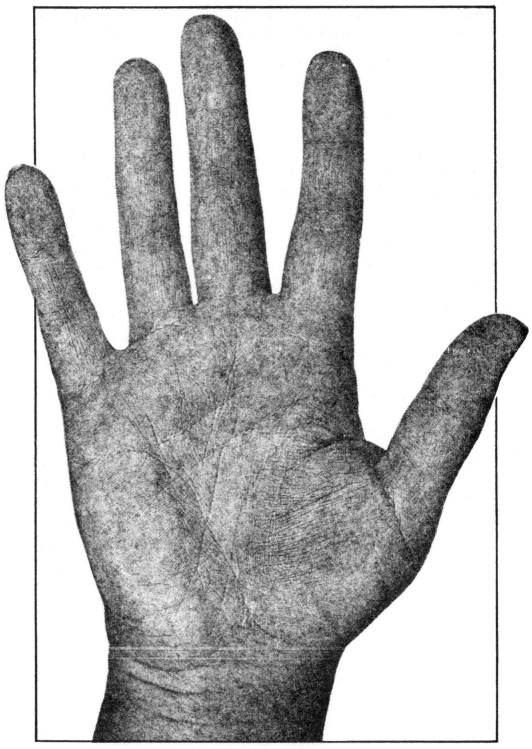

Fig. 36: A Two-Fated Palm (Cathie P.)

the line of life (6), it shows a dependency on the parents into adulthood. This is also shown when it springs from the Line of Life itself.

When it is far separated from the Line of Life (7) and travels from the wrist up, there is an early separation from the family.

A Two-Fated Palm

Cathie P., thirty-one (Fig. 36), whose palm is shown here as an example of a *double Line of Fate*, is a journalist at a Los Angeles-area newspaper. Her major duties are editing and layout, jobs she is very gifted at, as shown by the Line of Fate commencing on the Mount of Luna and running up the center of the hand toward Jupiter. However, coming from Luna, it also makes her dependent on the approval of others. An equally strong Line of Fate stems from the Line of Life and heads toward Apollo, giving her talent in the arts and the ability to make a living.

Her Line of Head is separated from the Line of Life, which makes her a risk-taker.

Therefore, the lady is loaded with talent and drive but will hold back her desires in order to please others—that is, until she's about forty. This is shown by another, smaller Line of Fate which starts from her Line of Head and ascends to the finger of Saturn.

Other markings to take note of are the long Line of Head, which makes her bright, and the long second phalange on the thumb, which makes her a very logical thinker. The first phalange on the thumb is quite short, compared to the second, showing that she lacks willpower.

As shown by this hand, palmistry doesn't foretell the future in exact terms. It only points out the potential. It sets the course, like a ship sailing from one port to another, but along the way the captain has to make numerous decisions.

CHAPTER SEVEN

Minor Lines of the Hand

THE MINOR LINES of the hand often tell separate tales of their own, or, when branching off main lines, flesh out the story of those markings.

THE LINES OF MARRIAGE AND RELATIONSHIP

Lines of Marriage and Relationship run *horizontally* down the little-finger side of the hand at the edge of the palm. Usually, Marriage Lines are above the Line of Heart and are stronger than the shorter liaisons shown farther down. Numerous lines running horizontally indicate a gregarious individual who has many friends as well as lovers.

Those lying above the Line of Heart and beneath the little finger tell the approximate age when the marriage or deep relationship occurs. A line high up, close to the bottom crease of the little finger, indicates a marriage before the age of twenty-five; midway, between twenty-five and forty. A line closer to the Line of Heart means the marriage occurs after the age of fifty-five.*

*See Appendix for more about determining ages.

If the Marriage and Relationship Line is as deep and strong as the major lines (chiefly the person's Line of Fate), their mate will dominate them.

When one Marriage and Relationship Line appears stronger than any of the others, it means that no matter whether the person has married several times or has had numerous liaisons, that one particular love affair has more meaning than the others.

Puffiness around one of the lines indicates unhappiness with that union. The swelling can disappear if the problem is taken care of, or if there is some type of separation—either short-term or permanent. The puffiness usually means that the person is holding back their emotions and suffering the consequences. *Deep red* lines indicate temporary anger at the partner and a *darkened* line shows depression originating from the relationship.

When the line curves upward (A) (see Fig. 37), these people would be better off remaining single. This doesn't mean that they aren't loving or capable of having a good relationship, but that they might ultimately feel stifled once the marriage license is signed.

If the line droops downward (B), the person's partner will die before them. Little *hairlines* drooping from the Marriage Line reveal that the partner will be ill frequently. A line with an *island* on it (C) indicates trouble with the marriage and a separation.

When the line ends in a fork (D), a divorce is imminent. This is also the case when the line breaks in the middle.

A line running vertically and cutting the Line of Marriage shows opposition to the union, usually by relatives.

If the union is strong, or has had a great impact (for good or bad) on the individual's life, there may be *backup lines* on the Mount of Venus (1).

When a fainter line runs closely parallel to a Marriage Line, it foretells an affair during that marriage (E).

I'm often asked at the beginning of a reading whether I see any affairs. Most who ask this question appear to be having trouble with their present marriage or relationship and acknowledge that they desire an affair. They apparently believe that having a new love is going to cure some of their problems.

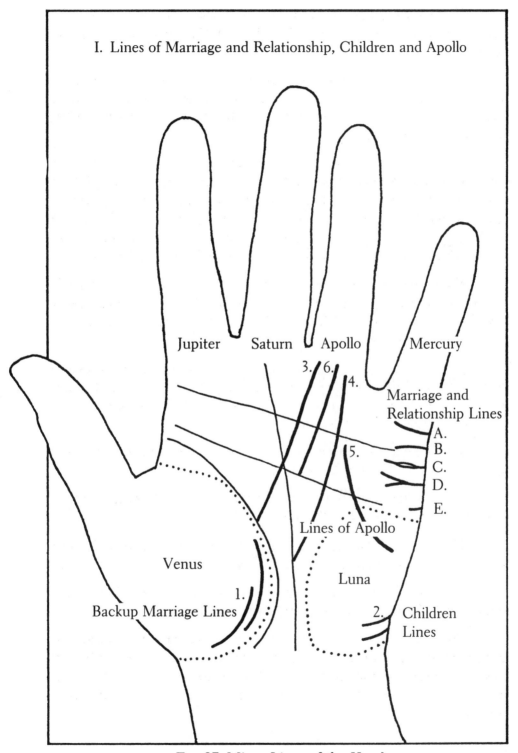

FIG. 37: Minor Lines of the Hand

A Strong Line of Marriage and Relationship

Despite the preponderance of unhappy marriages and troubled relationships, I've chosen to illustrate the Marriage Lines with a hand that has one good, strong marriage (Fig. 38).

The line is deep, clear and without breaks and, sure enough, Nancy M., sixty-three, has been married forty-one years to the same man she fell in love with prior to World War II. They had known one another since seventh grade and married when she was twenty-one.

"We still have a lot of fun and it seems like only two days ago when we got married," she said. From the looks of her hand, Nancy's innate personality would help account for this.

Her Line of Heart begins between Saturn and Jupiter, showing someone who accepts reality and makes few demands on a relationship. She is optimistic by nature. Furthermore, one of her Lines of Fate (she has more than one, which indicates multiple types of jobs) ends on the Mount of Luna, which makes her helpful to others. She trusts her intuition and sincerely cares about other people.

However, this Line of Fate arising from Luna makes her dependent on the approval of others, just as we saw with Cathie P. (Fig. 36).

THE LINES OF CHILDREN

Many palmists study vertical lines running upward from the Marriage Lines for signs of children. I have always found this a guessing game because the lines are very faint and may be interference lines.

I place more value on the deep lines running horizontally above the wrist on or near the Mount of Luna (2) (see Fig. 37). If Children Lines appear to spring upward from a Marriage Line but are unclear, they can be compared with the lines on the wrist for more certainty.

These lines most frequently appear on the hands of women, but if the father shares equally in the care and nurturing of the children (and there are a growing number of them today), he too may have these lines.

They don't always appear on parents' hands. This does not mean that they are any less caring about their offspring than those with the lines. These lines are simply a sort of bonus indicator of children.

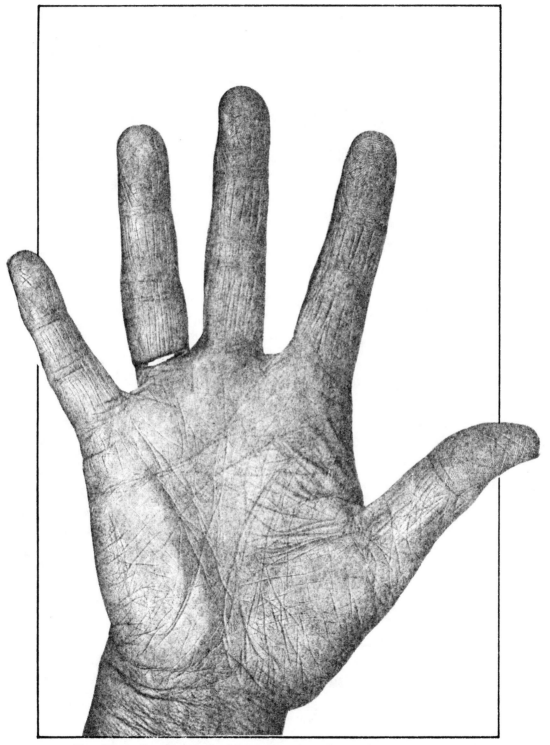

Fig. 38: A Strong Line of Marriage & Relationship (Nancy M.)

Straight lines running upward on the Marriage Lines are supposed to indicate boys and *slightly curved* ones, girls. However, I have never found this a good indicator. Neither are there any markings to determine sex on the lines near the Mount of Luna.

THE LINE OF APOLLO

The Line of Apollo runs vertically up the palm toward the finger of Apollo. It should not be confused with the Line of Fate and is usually fainter than Fate and farther from the Line of Life.

When the Line of Apollo rises from the Line of Life (3) (see Fig. 37), it lends itself to artistic pursuits.

Rising from a strong, well-developed line of fate (4), it promises success.

When it stems from the Mount of Luna (5), success is dependent on the help of others, unless the Line of Head slopes toward this mount. In that case, it belongs to the hand of a writer.

When its origin is the Line of Head (6), it promises success after forty, especially if the line is forked.

Some people have numerous Lines of Apollo springing from all directions but terminating on the Mount of Apollo. Unfortunately, though they may be talented, their ideas are too scattered in too many directions to achieve a full measure of success.

Overall, people with Lines of Apollo tend to lead more exciting, if riskier lives, than those without. The line happens to be one of my favorites; when it appears, I know that person's life will never be dull.

THE LINE OF HEALTH

The Line of Health (1) (see Fig. 39) usually descends from the Mount of Mercury and terminates at various locations, giving clues to the person's propensity toward health.

It's best not to have this line at all. Its purpose is to warn of potential health problems, and the longer the line, the greater the potential for danger.

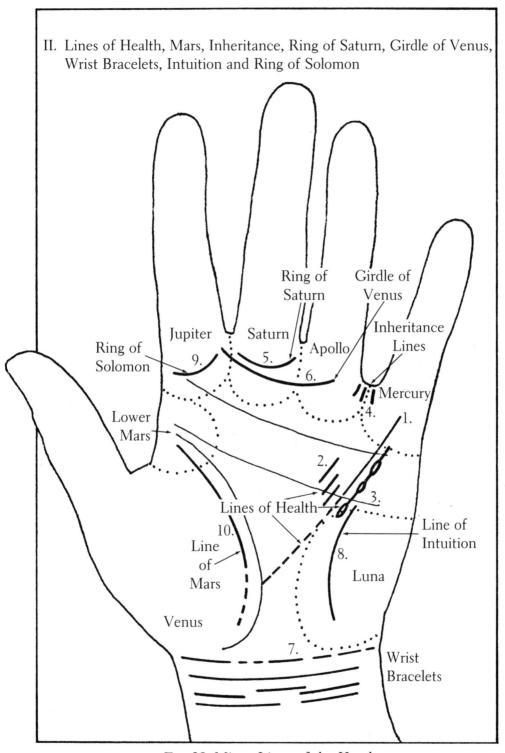

II. Lines of Health, Mars, Inheritance, Ring of Saturn, Girdle of Venus, Wrist Bracelets, Intuition and Ring of Solomon

FIG. 39: Minor Lines of the Hand

It can travel down from Mercury and touch the Line of Life, which signifies serious health problems if the Line of Life is *weaker after the point of juncture*. It usually denotes cardiovascular disease, often of an hereditary nature.

If such a line appears, check the left hand to see if it is indeed hereditary. If it is, it will also show up on the left hand.

If either of the person's parents has a history of heart disease, precautionary steps should be taken by the person to guard against it happening to them—careful diet, no cigarettes, exercise, regular checkups.

Other Health Aspects

If the Line of Health is *reddish* in color, it signifies too much poison in the body, such as alcohol, nicotine, refined sugar or environmental toxins.

When the line is wavy, it tells of kidney and bladder problems.

If it is formed by a number of straight, short lines (2), it means stomach problems such as ulcers.

When chained, or made up of little islands (3), lung disease may eventually be a problem.

Having any of these formations doesn't guarantee that the disease will strike, but the potential is there to a greater degree than for those who don't have these signs.

An Unusual Health Line

The following palm-print (Fig. 40) illustrates an unusual formation of Health Lines in the darkened area situated near the center of the palm. It is not a fortunate sign, but the hands are interesting and so is their owner, Mary N.

Although this dark area dominates the hand, indicating a struggle with health, the Lines of Life and Fate are strong and continue for many years.

It is a delicate, small hand with an unusually large thumb for the hand size. The thumb lends an enormous amount of strength and character to the hand. Additionally, Lower Mars appears creased and puffy, which means this person can tolerate an unusual amount of physical pain.

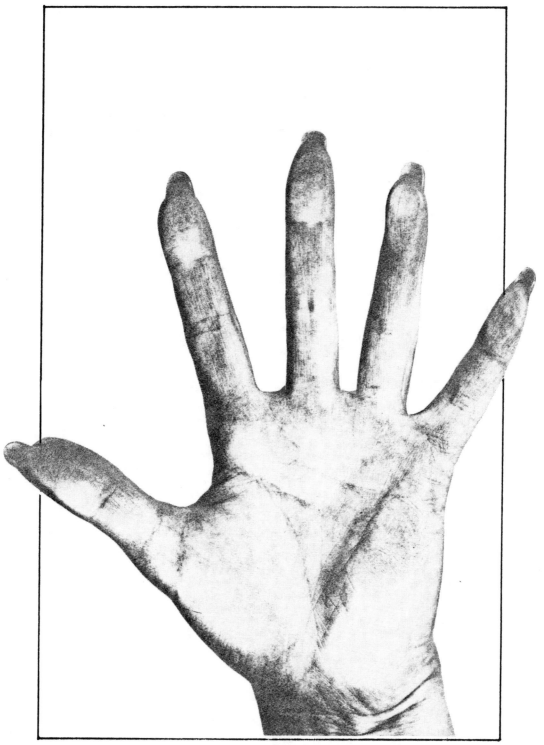

Fig. 40: An Unusual Health Line (Mary N.)

And indeed she has. More than five years ago, Mary, then forty-two, was diagnosed as having terminal cancer and given two months to a year to live, even with chemotherapy. Following a mastectomy, the cancer had spread to other parts of her body, including the liver.

To beat the odds, she combined traditional cancer therapy with holistic and New-Age philosophies. Mary, holder of two master's degrees, is a speech pathologist, but during the treatment process, she lost her job. Her income dwindled to $100 per month—child support from a husband who had deserted her and her daughter sixteen years previously.

Several fund-raisers at the school where Mary had taught for nearly twenty years helped her stay on her feet until disability payments started. The fund-raisers also helped her to travel and meet with Dr. Elisabeth Kubler-Ross, credited with enlightening Americans about the dying process; Dr. Brugh Joy, a leader in the holistic health movement; and Olga Worrall (now deceased), considered by many to be the greatest healer of her time.

Today, Mary works with the hospice movement, is a noted lecturer and teaches part time.

Another interesting formation on her hand is the long finger of Jupiter, which is nearly as long as the middle finger and much longer than the ring finger. This is the sign of a leader.

THE LINE OF MARS

The Line of Mars (10) runs from the Mount of Lower Mars inside the Line of Life. This Mars Line is a backup which protects the person's health when there are breaks in the Line of Life. Don't confuse this line with the Backup Marriage Lines (1) (see Fig. 37).

ADDITIONAL MINOR LINES

INHERITANCE LINES

These lines are those little hash marks appearing between the finger of Mercury and Apollo (4) (see Fig. 39). They promise money or goods, although the amount is not indicated.

The Ring of Saturn

This is an unlucky sign. It is found just beneath the middle finger (5) and diminishes the success of the person because they have a tendency not to complete what they start.

The Girdle of Venus

This line runs beneath the fingers and above the Line of Heart (6). It adds a sensual nature to those who have it. It will be a much fainter and finer line than the major lines. People with this mark (it is not frequently found) can be very sensitive but are difficult to get along with. Their expectations of themselves and others are great. Rarely, you may see numerous Girdles of Venus; they are found on the hands of super-sensitive people.

The Wrist Bracelets

These lines, lying on the inside of the wrist (7), have long been associated with longevity if they are unbroken. I have never found this to be true. I've seen the hands of eighty-five-year-old women whose bracelets look like Chicago road maps.

The only significance I give them is if the top one curves into the palm. On a woman's hand this indicates a difficult time giving birth.

The Line of Intuition

This is that curved line found on the Mount of Luna (8). It has long been associated with those whose lives are involved in the occult or spiritual sciences. However, I have known many sensitives, spiritualists and those who use their intuition on a deeper level who do not have this marking.

I most often find it on the hands of people who take risks with the decisions they make in their lives. They're untroubled by following uncharted paths.

The Ring of Solomon

This line is a semicircle found at the base of the finger of Jupiter (9) and denotes a teacher or master of spiritual sciences. I have also found it on the hands of therapists and counselors who have adopted Eastern religions into their lives. People with this marking have little interest in the material aspects of life.

TRAVEL LINES

These lines (see Fig. 41) are found branching off from Luna (1) or rising from the bracelets of the wrist (2). They tend to be wispy unless the journey has a major impact on the person's life. Travel lines are only indicative of major or long trips, usually across water.

How they terminate, as they sweep into the palm, tells you something about their outcome. The longer or deeper the line, the more significant the journey.

Lines that end in an *island* (A) indicate an unhappy journey. If they end in a *square* (B), the person will be protected from some imminent danger. If they end in a *cross* (C), the trip will be disappointing.

Most travel lines, however, do not have these ominous endings, although I have encountered a few, chiefly the (A) variation.

A TRAVELING LADY

The following handprint (Fig. 42) belongs to Judy H., a forty-five-year-old single mother and school teacher who turned down a marriage proposal in her twenties for a chance to teach in foreign countries.

After teaching stints in Nepal, Japan, Greece and Mexico, she returned with her adopted daughter, Tasha, and settled into a teacher's job in Los Angeles County.

As can be seen from her palm, this lady loves to travel. It is a restlessness within her that will never go away, as shown by the deep Line of Travel curving over from Luna and touching a Line of Fate that heads toward Mercury.

In addition to that Line of Fate, another runs up the middle of the palm toward Saturn. It has a forked beginning, which shows a restless nature. The Line of Life also forks, adding to the wanderlust that is inherent in her character. Notice also the little Lines of Travel rising from the wrist and crossing the Mount of Luna.

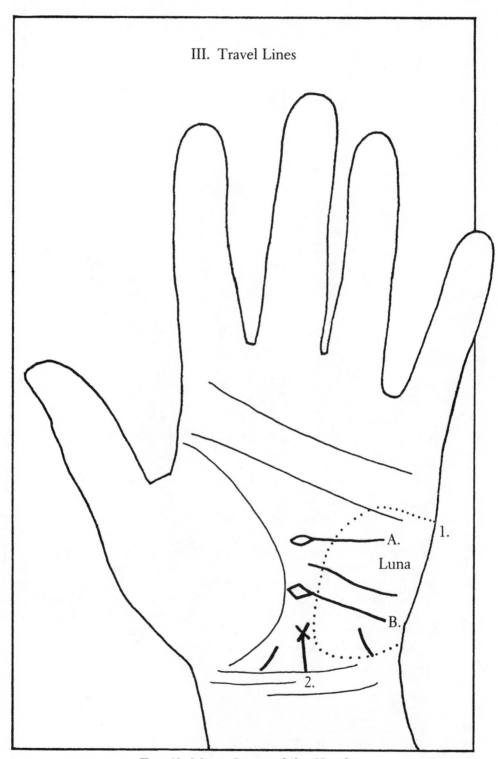

III. Travel Lines

A. Luna

B.

1.

2.

FIG. 41: Minor Lines of the Hand

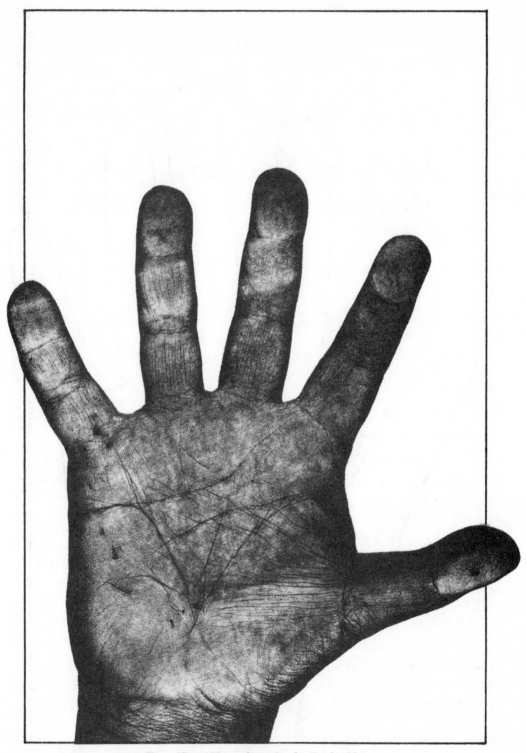

Fig. 42: A Traveling Lady (Judy H.)

CHAPTER EIGHT

Additional Significant Markings

THE GRILLE

The Grille (see Fig. 43), a crisscrossing of small lines, miminizes the potential of any mount it appears on.

In one instance, though, when it appears on the Mount of Jupiter (1), it's a good sign, especially if Jupiter is excessively long and the mount well developed. This is the sign of a leader, but one who could easily go too far in their demands if the Grille wasn't there to calm them down.

Most of the people I've seen with this mark have management capabilities, but have learned to temper their overriding forcefulness. When I've pointed this out to them, they are aware of their drive and strength and acknowledge that they have purposely checked it in order to work well with others.

A Grille on the Mount of Apollo diminishes some of the person's artistic capabilities because it scatters their energies. On Saturn it takes away some of the person's charm. On Mercury it causes bad decisions in money matters, and on Luna it diminishes some of the imagination.

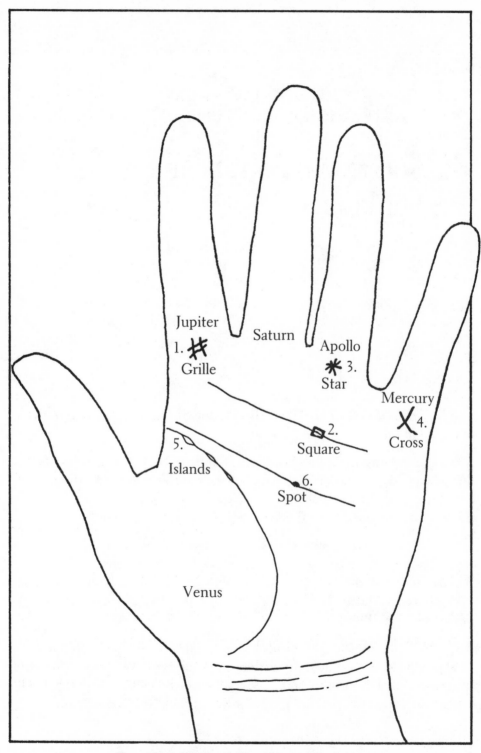

Fig. 43: Additional Significant Markings

THE SQUARE

The Square is a mark of protection on the lines or mounts on which it appears. Often it is a protection against the ill will of others.

Thus, if it appears on the Line of Heart (2), it will protect the person from heartbreak; on Mercury and the Line of Fate, from financial loss; on Venus, from excess passion; on the Line of Head, from emotional problems; on the Line of Life, from death; on Jupiter, from notoriety; and on Saturn, from morbidity.

THE STAR

The Star is supposed to be one of the most fortunate signs to have. It promises success in whatever area it falls. I have seldom found a Star on anyone's hand. I've seen what might have been a Star if I had used my imagination, since this mark is made up of a crisscross of lines. But such a mark would seem to indicate that regardless of what a person does, they are destined for success from the outset. I prefer to have several different markings indicate success as an outgrowth of the person's own character and hard work, rather than relying on only one rather dubious sign. People may be born with silver spoons in their mouths, but they still have to learn how to feed themselves with them.

However, I will list the meanings of the Star in case you ever run into it.:

On the Mount of Apollo (3) it indicates fame and fortune, possibly as an actor.

On the Mount of Mercury, it provides success in business, finance or the sciences.

On the Mount of Lower Mars, it indicates military success.

On the Mount of Venus, it brings success in love.

On the fingers, it brings success in whatever is attempted regarding the meaning of that mount. For example, if the Star appears on Jupiter, success in management.

THE CROSS

The Cross, wherever it is found, is an ominous sign.

On Venus it brings trouble with the affections.

On Saturn it can cause a physical accident.

On Apollo it can mean failure at artistic pursuits.

On Mercury (4) it is the sign of a liar.

Touching the Line of Head, it means an injury to the head.

ISLANDS

Islands usually appear within or at the ends of lines or on the mounts. They are signs of trouble, but not permanent ones.

An Island on the mounts of the hand takes away from the qualities of that mount: for example, on Apollo it diminishes artistic talents; on Jupiter it weakens leadership; on Mercury it thwarts financial success; and on Luna it indicates a person easily influenced by others.

On the Line of Life (5), it indicates illness at the point where it occurs. When little Islands or chains appear in the first part of the Line of Life, lying under Jupiter, I have found that it shows problems with the female organs.

On the Line of Fate, they indicate problems with the career.

On the Line of Apollo, they mean a possible scandal.

On the Line of Health, they can indicate serious illness.

SPOTS

Spots on the hand also indicate temporary problems, but usually concerning health. *Dark* spots show emotional illness, especially when they appear on the Line of Head (6). *Red* spots indicate fever.

TYPES OF LINES

Hands that are covered with a network of tiny lines show lack of direction. Depending on other lines and formations, however, the person may ultimately be very successful, but usually not until past mid-life.

Lines that are *red* show an active life with a good flow of energy. When the lines have a *yellow* tinge to them, the person is reserved and sometimes timid. If the lines are extremely *dark*, the person tends to be morbid.

Lines are usually *fainter* on conic, philosophic and psychic hands and appear *deeper* on spatulate, square and mixed hands.

Forked lines (A) (see Fig. 44) have additional power.

Wavy (B), *tasseled* (C), *chained* (D) or *broken* lines (E) diminish the strength of the line. If a line is broken, look for a *Backup* line next to it (F).

HEALER'S MARKS

Healer's Marks are short lines found on the Mount of Mercury and don't necessarily belong to physicians (G). Rather, they are found on the hands of people who seem to attract others to them simply because it feels good to be around them.

They are usually demonstrative people who find it natural to hug both male and female acquaintances. They are good listeners, and after leaving their presence, a person feels better.

Often, they are unaware of their talents, and can be found in unlikely professions. The only drawback to these markings is that people who have them tend to attract those who become dependent on them.

A Hand with Healer's Marks

The following hand, which contains Healer's Marks (Fig. 45), belongs to Dorothy S., a realtor in a small mountain community whose clients often return for visits just to chat after they've bought or rented a house from her.

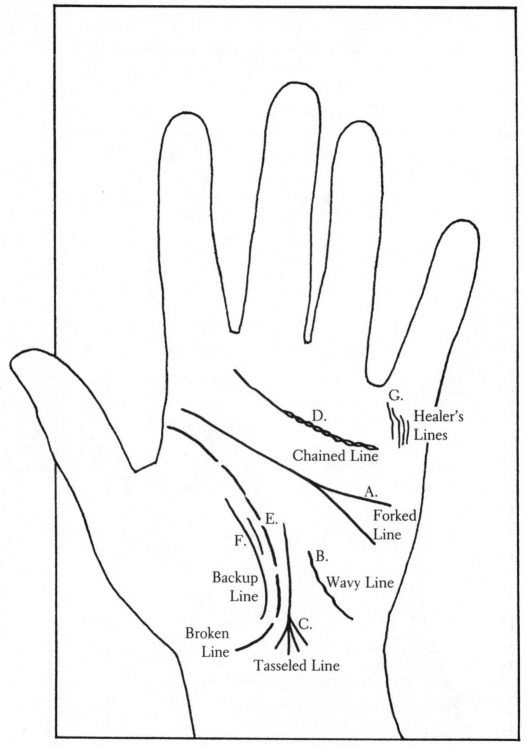

FIG. 44: Types of Lines

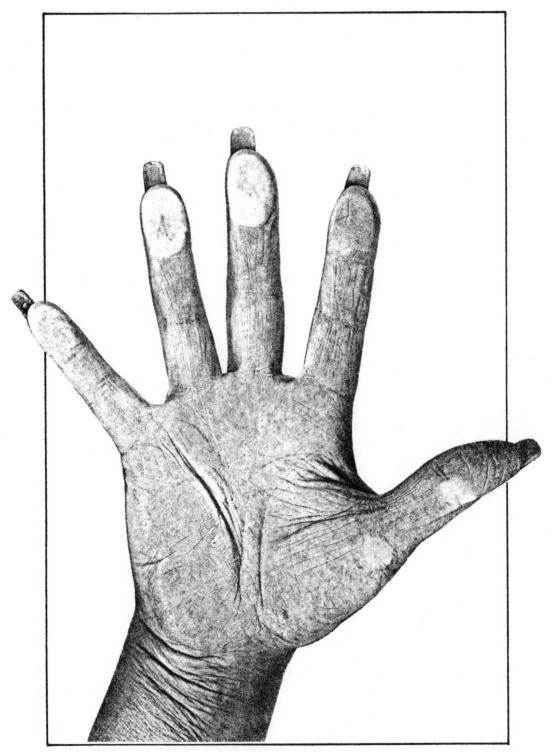

FIG. 45: A Hand with Healer's Marks (Dorothy S.)

APPENDIX

Determining Time

UNLESS YOU'RE PSYCHIC, the age of a person when a certain event has taken place or is going to take place is not that clearly indicated by the palm. The more hands you read, however, the more fine-tuning you can do regarding time. It comes easily only with experience.

Following are some charts to help you navigate toward the approximate age of a person when an event is likely to occur.

TIME AS SEEN ON THE LINE OF LIFE

Example (A) (see Fig. 46) shows two hairlines springing from the Line of Life and heading toward Jupiter. They indicate the furthering of an education between the ages of twenty-five and thirty.

Example (B) shows an Island farther down on the palm, indicating an illness at about age forty-five.

TIME AS SEEN ON THE MARRIAGE LINES

Marriage Lines (see Fig. 47) begin with the earliest years closest to the little finger (A) and travel downward with age. Midway between the

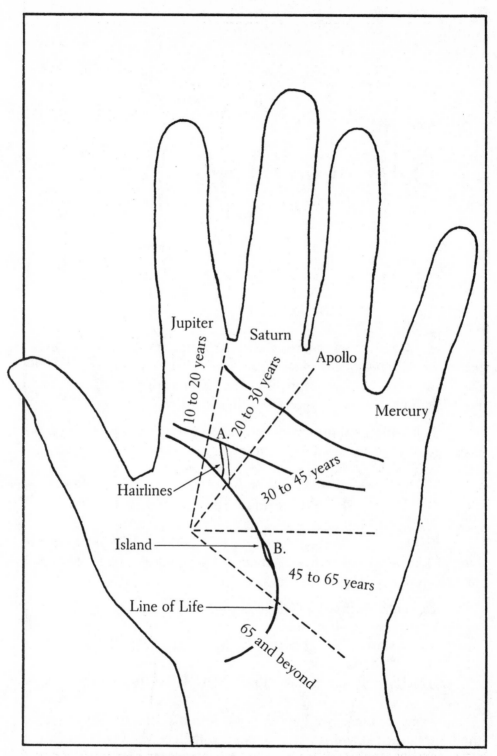

FIG. 46: Time as Seen on the Line of Life

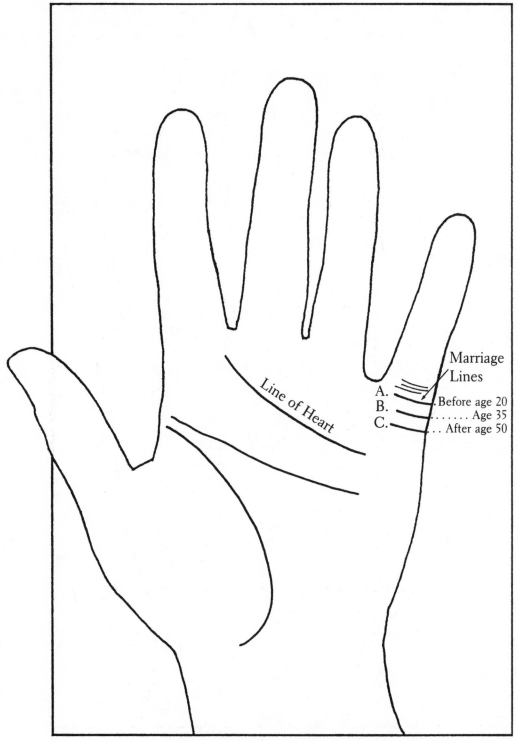

FIG. 47: Time as Seen on the Marriage Lines

crease of the little finger and the Line of Heart (B) would be about age thirty-five. Three-quarters of the way down (C) would be after age fifty.

TIME AS SEEN ON THE LINE OF FATE

Branches (A) and (B) on Fig. 48, which focuses on the Line of Fate, involve career changes. The first career change (A) falls into the twenty-to-thirty-year age group. The second career change occurs in the forty-five-to-sixty-year age group.

Fig. 49 illustrates a late start with a career, so the ages are read differently. If the Line of Fate doesn't begin until the middle of the palm, the time periods are indicated as shown.

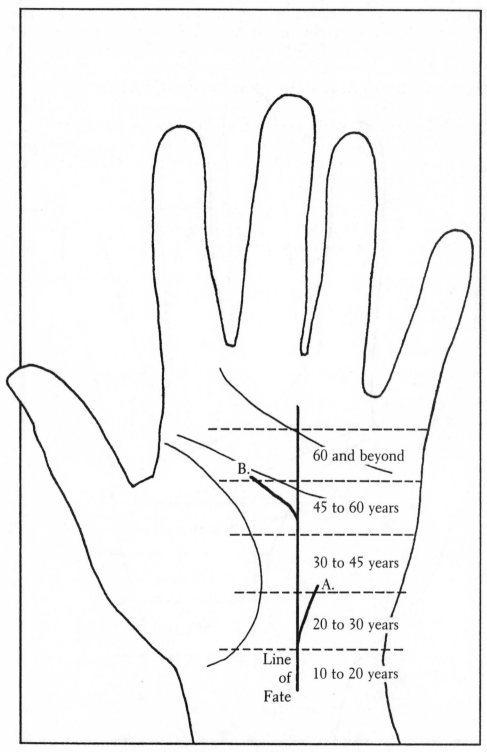

Fig. 48: Time as Seen on the Line of Fate I

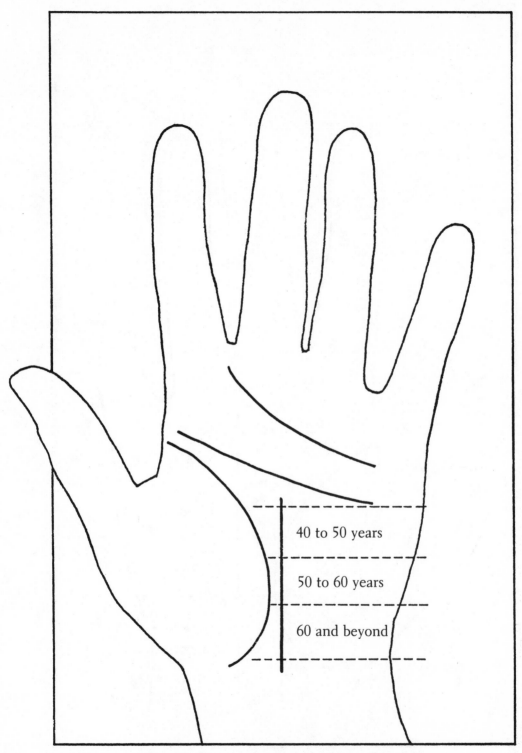

FIG. 49: Time as Seen on the Line of Fate II